A Noteworthy Americans
Quick Reader Biography Book

Wolves in Blue

Stories of
the North Brothers and Their Pawnee Scouts

by Jean A. Lukesh

Field Mouse
PRODUCTIONS

Grand Island/Palmer, NE

No part of this publication may be reproduced, or stored in a retrieval system, or transmitted in any form or by any means, electronic, mechanical, photocopying, recording, or otherwise, without the permission in writing from the publisher/author.

Copyright © 2011 Jean A. Lukesh
Cover and maps copyright ©2011 by Ronald E. Lukesh

Published by Field Mouse Productions
Grand Island and Palmer, Nebraska
All rights reserved
First Printed, December 2011
Printed in the United States of America
Maps by Ron Lukesh.
This Noteworthy Americans Quick Reader biography was designed
For young readers ages 10 to 110
by Jean A. Lukesh (Ed.D., Curriculum & Instruction).
R.L.: 7.5   I.L.: grade 4.6 through adult

Lukesh, Jean A., 1950—
Wolves in Blue: Stories of the North Brothers and Their Pawnee Scouts
SUMMARY: A young adult quick reading biography of brothers Frank and Luther North and their Pawnee Scouts who worked with the U.S. Army to protect and rescue overland trail travelers, settlers, soldiers, and Union Pacific railroad workers across the Great Plains during the Plains Indian Wars and the building of the Transcontinental Railroad. Two of those Pawnee Scouts "shared" the first Congressional Medal of Honor ever awarded to a Native American.
Includes photographs, timeline, index, select bibliographical references, critical thinking questions, glossary, and bold vocabulary terms in the text.
Noteworthy Americans Quick Reader Biography Series
1. Frank J. North, 1840-1885—Biography—Juvenile. 2. Luther H. North, 1846-1935—History. 3. Indians of North America—Wars—1866-1895. 4. Pawnee Indians. 5. Nebraska—History. 6. Soldiers—History—19th Century. 7. Transcontinental Railroad—History. 8. United States—Armed Forces—Americans. 9. Frontier and Pioneer Life—West—U.S. 10. Overland Trails—West—U.S. 11. Scouting (Reconnaissance). 12. Union Pacific Railroad—History. I. Title.   II. Subtitle.   III. Series.
E 83.866   970.06 [B]   [920] [921]   ISBN 978-0-9647586-4-3

Front Cover: White Horse, a Pawnee Scout Back Cover: Four Pawnee Scouts (Photos Courtesy Nebraska State Historical Society)

Note: Terms written in Bold type in the text that are not chapter headings or section headings are vocabulary glossary terms.

This book is dedicated to
the memory of Frank and Luther North,
and their officers and families, the Arnolds,
the Morses, the Cushings, James Murie Sr. and Jr.,
Charles Small, Gus Becher, Fred Matthews, Isaac Davis,
William Harvey, William Rudy, William Lee, and more,
Gen. Sam Curtis, Buffalo Bill Cody, and C.S. Mienhall;
and, of course, to the hundreds of heroic Pawnee Scouts
of Nebraska and Oklahoma in the 1860s and 1870s,
including the two "Bear" scouts who "shared" the
Congressional Medal of Honor in 1869,
the first such medal ever given to a Native American,
as well as to patriotic Pawnee veterans and their families
whose tribal flag now shows several arrowheads—
one for each and every war in which Pawnee
warriors/soldiers have fought for the U.S.A.—
from the Plains Indian Wars to the wars of present day.
Also to good friends Mick Starns (of the North family),
Theodore "Teeter" Morgan of the Knife Chief family,
Geraldine Howells and Irene Edwards,
Ted Reeves who introduced me to Pawnee history,
Roger Welsch (my Pawnee-Omaha-Wannabe friend),
Gale and Peggy of the Pawnee Arts Center,
Ronnie O'Brien of the Kearney Archway,
Gary Zaruba of MONA, Nancy and Jerry Carlson of the
Genoa Indian School, the Russells, the Boltes,
and many others from Hall, Howard, Merrick
and Nance, Counties (NE) and Pawnee (OK),
and my "mountain man" friend Maurice Paulk.
****

In very broken-Pawnee, I humbly say to all of them:
Too a hay. I way too a hay. Rawa iri.
Tucikstawawa?u-ki. Wera-ta.
Ee wa wat oo soo koo.
Nowa/Nowwa/Na'wah/Nawa!
****

Timeline for North Brothers and Pawnee Scouts

1700s	Pawnee are powerful longtime residents in Nebraska area
1803	President Jefferson buys Louisiana Territory
1804	Lewis and Clark explore the Louisiana Territory
1833	Treaty buys Pawnee land south of Platte River
1836	Oregon Trail Traffic begins along Platte Valley
1839	James E. (J.E.) North born in New York state
1840	Mar 10, Frank J. North born in New York state
1846	Mar 6, Luther "Lute" H. North born in Ohio state
1848	Government treaty buys Pawnee land along Platte River from Fort Kearny to the eastern end of the Grand Island
1849-50	California Trail Traffic starts across the Platte Valley
1854	Kansas-Nebraska Act passes, opens land to settlement
1855-56	North family. moves to Omaha; Frank meets Gen. Dodge
1857	Winter, Father North freezes to death while surveying
1857	Treaty of Table Creek, Pawnee have only Loup River land; agree to move to new Reservation there
1858	Norths and Arnolds move to Columbus area
1859	J.E. in Army; Lute rides mail route; Pawnee War; Pawnee make the move to Reservation on Loup River
1860	Frank works at Pawnee Reservation store
1860-75	Enemy tribes make raids on Pawnee Reservation
1861	April, Civil War starts back East
1862	Santee raids, Minnesota/Dakotas; Lute in Nebraska Cavalry
1862	Government passes Homestead Act and Railroad Acts
1864	Plains Indian Wars start; Pawnee Scout experiment begins
1865	Second Pawnee Scouts; Powder River War in Wyoming; Civil War ends; Union Pacific Railroad (UPRR) starts west
1866	UPRR at 100th Meridian; Plum Creek and other attacks
1867	Guarding General Sherman; Plum Creek Railroad Attack
1868	Republican River War in Kansas
1869	Transcontinental Railroad completed; Cody with Scouts; Battle of Summit Springs; "Bear" wins Medal of Honor
1873	Trenton Massacre/Massacre Canyon
1874	Pawnee begin migration to Oklahoma
1876	Last group of Pawnee Scouts; Red Cloud's War
1877	Pawnee Scouts end; Cody-North Cattle Ranch begins
1882	Frank North elected to Nebraska legislature
1883	Cody's Wild West Show features Pawnee Scouts
1884	Frank North injured by horse at Wild West Show
1885	March 14, Frank North dies, buried in Columbus, NE
1935	April 18, Luther North dies; buried in Columbus, NE

Table of Contents

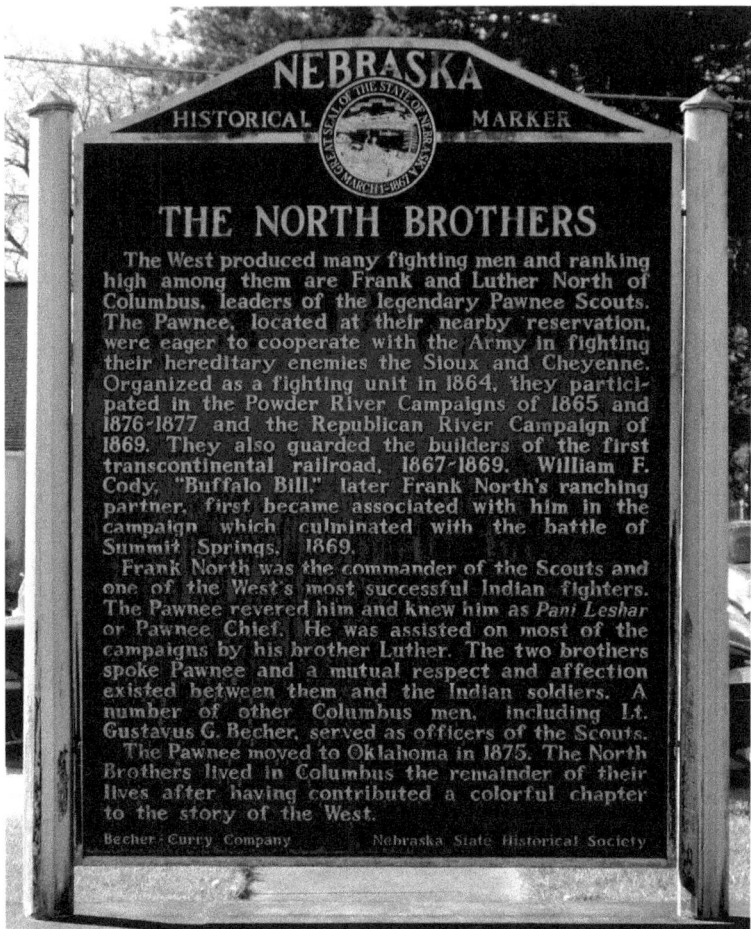

NEBRASKA

HISTORICAL MARKER

THE NORTH BROTHERS

The West produced many fighting men and ranking high among them are Frank and Luther North of Columbus, leaders of the legendary Pawnee Scouts. The Pawnee, located at their nearby reservation, were eager to cooperate with the Army in fighting their hereditary enemies the Sioux and Cheyenne. Organized as a fighting unit in 1864, they participated in the Powder River Campaigns of 1865 and 1876-1877 and the Republican River Campaign of 1869. They also guarded the builders of the first transcontinental railroad, 1867-1869. William F. Cody, "Buffalo Bill," later Frank North's ranching partner, first became associated with him in the campaign which culminated with the battle of Summit Springs, 1869.

Frank North was the commander of the Scouts and one of the West's most successful Indian fighters. The Pawnee revered him and knew him as *Pani Leshar* or Pawnee Chief. He was assisted on most of the campaigns by his brother Luther. The two brothers spoke Pawnee and a mutual respect and affection existed between them and the Indian soldiers. A number of other Columbus men, including Lt. Gustavus G. Becher, served as officers of the Scouts.

The Pawnee moved to Oklahoma in 1875. The North Brothers lived in Columbus the remainder of their lives after having contributed a colorful chapter to the story of the West.

Becher-Curry Company   Nebraska State Historical Society

The North Brothers historical marker located on the Chamber of Commerce lawn in Columbus, Nebraska, the hometown of the North Brothers.   (Photo by Ron Lukesh)

Chapter 1:

Meeting the "Wolf People"

In 1856, when they were sixteen- and ten-years old, brothers Frank and Luther North traveled by railroad, stagecoach, and wagon to the newly opened wilderness of Nebraska Territory. There, they not only learned to survive in the Plains wilderness, but to **thrive** in it.

Shortly after moving to a log cabin near the new town of Omaha, the boys and their family made friends with their neighbors. Those neighbors included three families of friendly Pawnee Indians—or the "People of the Wolf"—who were camped nearby.

The boys did not know it yet, but that early

North-Pawnee friendship was just the start of a strong and respectful relationship that would last many lifetimes—through years of war and peace.

The lives of the North brothers would forever be tied to the Pawnee and to people heading west by horses, wagons, stagecoaches, and the railroad.

As they grew, Frank, Luther, and their older brother James (or J.E.) moved west. They worked hard and built a strong reputation for honesty, trustworthiness, and good character wherever they went.

The U.S. Army called upon them to act as guides, scouts, or volunteer soldiers when needed. They were liked and respected among their own people and by the Pawnee, as well.

The Norths learned the language and customs of the Pawnee and often interacted with them. They also proved their bravery when they crossed paths with the more **hostile** western Plains Indians, the longtime enemies of the Pawnee.

During the Plains Indian troubles of the

1860s, the U.S. government even tried an experiment with them. The government hired Frank North to select and lead Pawnee men to work as scouts for the U.S. Army—or the "bluecoats," as the Plains Indians often called the Army men and their uniforms.

Wearing Army bluecoats of their own, those scouts then tracked, hunted, and sometimes fought their old enemies—the hostile western tribes of the Sioux (now often called the Lakota), the Cheyenne, and the Arapaho.

Those Pawnee Scouts became known as "wolves for the bluecoats" or "wolves in blue," and that experiment worked well.

Few people today know who the Pawnee Scouts were. But during those years of the Plains Indian Wars of the 1860s and 1870s, Frank and Luther North and their Pawnee Scouts became heroes.

They saved the lives of hundreds of travelers, settlers, transcontinental railroad workers, soldiers, and even friendly Plains Indians. They did that along the overland trails and rails of Nebraska and across a vast area of the Central Plains, from Montana to Minnesota and from Canada to Kansas.

Two of the Pawnee Scouts even earned and shared the first Congressional Medal of Honor ever given to a Native American.

Here are just a few of the many amazing adventures of those heroes, the North brothers and their Pawnee Scouts—the Wolves in Blue.

Pawnee people at an earthlodge village
along the Loup River near Genoa, Nebraska, around 1870
(Photo Courtesy Nebraska State Historical Society)

Chapter 2

The Land and People of the Wolf

The Pawnee lived in what is now Nebraska for hundreds of years before the North family moved there. In those early days, explorers and frontiersmen knew the Pawnee as the first farmers of the Plains and as "the People of the Wolf."

The Skidi (Skee dee) or Wolf band of the Pawnee probably lived there first. For centuries, they often lived along or near the **Loup River.**

In the Pawnee language, the word Skidi meant wolf. The word Loup (loop) also meant wolf in the language of the French fur trappers who traded and sometimes lived with the Pawnee.

In the sign language of the Plains, the hand

sign for Pawnee and the sign for wolf were also very similar. For all those reasons and more, the Pawnee were called the People of the Wolf.

The Four Bands of the PAWNEE

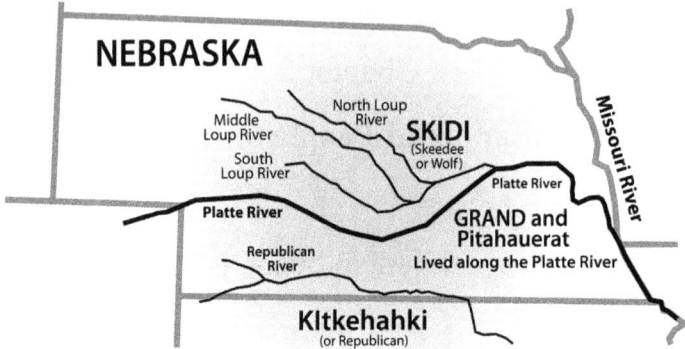

NEBRASKA

Middle Loup River

North Loup River

South Loup River

SKIDI (Skeedee or Wolf)

Platte River

Platte River

GRAND and Pitahauerat Lived along the Platte River

Republican River

Missouri River

Kitkehahki (or Republican)

Hunting lands of the four bands of the Pawnee and the major rivers where they often lived, showing the current borders of Nebraska and northern Kansas   (Map by Ron Lukesh)

Then There Were Four

Over the years, three other bands of Pawnee moved north and joined the Skidi in today's Nebraska and Kansas. They probably came from what is now Oklahoma. As a group, those three new ones were called the **Southband** Pawnee.

They had many names for their three bands, such as the **Grand**, the **Pitahauerat** (Pit uh how er rat), and the **Republican** or Kitkehahki (Kit kuh hawk kee) Pawnee.

The Skidi and the three Southband Pawnee groups all lived in large earthlodge villages or towns. They often lived along the Loup, Platte, and Republican Rivers in Nebraska and Kansas.

All four Pawnee bands spoke a similar language and shared many of the same customs.

They all farmed and raised corn, beans, pumpkins, and squash. They hunted buffalo twice a year and lived in tipis (or teepees) when on the hunting trails.

Together, the four bands formed the Pawnee Nation or Tribe, with 10,000 to 12,500 people. In those days, they were a very powerful group of people—farmers, hunters, and warriors.

Fighting Over Hunting Lands

The Pawnee needed to be powerful. They had many long-time enemies, especially the Sioux (now called the Lakota), the Cheyenne, and the Arapaho.

Those three **nomadic** tribes from the west

often banded together to live or hunt or fight their enemies. They become very powerful, too.

All of those Plains Indians needed to hunt large numbers of buffalo (or bison) as part of their religion and for their main meat source. Often, the three nomadic tribes and the Pawnee were deadly enemies on those hunting grounds.

Yet, those same Pawnee were often friendly to white people. Explorers, trappers, traders, mountain men, and military men often visited the Pawnee during the 1700s and early 1800s.

Their maps marked that vast hunting area as Pawnee land. Their reports said the Pawnee were mighty people and fearsome warriors who often ruled the Central Plains.

But that would soon change.

The Louisiana Purchase

In those early days, other countries (including Spain and France) sometimes claimed the lands where the Pawnee and other Plains Indians lived, too.

In 1803, President Thomas Jefferson bought all that land from France. He called that area the Louisiana **Territory**. By buying that land, Jefferson more than doubled the size of the new United States.

The next year, 1804, President Jefferson sent Meriwether Lewis and William Clark to explore that huge area of land. Jefferson wanted to know about the Native Americans who lived there and about other things, too.

Those explorers met very few Pawnee on their trip up the Missouri River in 1804 or down it in 1806. The Pawnee usually lived farther west on the Plains.

The Louisiana Territory Changes Its Name

In 1812, that huge Louisiana Territory was renamed Missouri Territory when an area of land down south became the new state of Louisiana.

Over the years, other parts of that big Missouri Territory were marked off, too. They became smaller territories or states as people began moving west.

In the mid-1850s, the northern part of that Louisiana/Missouri Territory would become Nebraska and Kansas Territories.

Chapter 3

The Westward Movement

In the late 1840s and the 1850s, the upper half of that Missouri Territory was still a wilderness of Plains Indian lands. However, wagon train trails had already begun to stretch across there, as many people from the Eastern United States began to travel west.

The new travelers went west along the broad Platte River and along other trails and rivers there. They followed the pathways of Plains Indians, trappers and traders, mountain men, explorers, military men, and missionaries.

In Search of Better Things

Some of those new people coming west were

just traveling through. Others came to stay.

Some rode horses. Others drove covered wagons or freight wagons, or they pulled **handcarts**. They came alone, or with families, or with other groups of people.

They came in search of a better life. Some came through on their way to find land in Oregon or gold in California. Some came west to find religious freedom in Utah or gold in Colorado. Some of them broke down along the way and built businesses or towns near the trails.

Several different overland trails ran across that land. They ran somewhat parallel to each other. They had many different names—the Oregon Trail, the California Trail, the California Cut-off, the Mormon Trail, and others.

Over the years, thousands of people traveled those roadways. They brought new tools, weapons, and lifestyles. They also brought different ways of thinking and several new and deadly diseases.

Those people, too, used the hunting lands of

the Pawnee and other Plains Indians. So, as they moved, they feared for their own safety. They wanted and demanded protection for their families, their covered wagons, and their animals.

They had much to be afraid of—the weather, accidents, sickness, dangerous river crossings, wild animals, hostile Plains Indians, and more.

Missouri Territory Splits in Two

In the mid-1850s, more and more people from the East began moving into or across Missouri Territory, where the Plains Indians lived.

Even though that territory was huge, the overland trails that crossed the center of that land intruded a lot on the Plains Indians and their ways of life.

In those early days, the Missouri Territory was too big an area of wilderness to try to control or protect, especially with so many new people moving across it. That area needed to be split.

The Kansas-Nebraska Act of 1854

Partly for those reasons but mostly for other

political reasons, the government back east passed the Kansas-Nebraska Act in 1854.

That act formed two smaller territories out of the top half of the big Missouri Territory. Those new territories were then given the names Kansas and Nebraska—but they looked very different from today's Kansas and Nebraska.

That new Nebraska Territory was so big that all of today's state of Nebraska and parts of the future states of Colorado, Wyoming, Montana, and North and South Dakota fit inside it.

The new Kansas Territory, just to the south of Nebraska Territory, was so big it included all of today's state of Kansas and part of Colorado.

People from the East were already traveling through those territories. The Kansas-Nebraska Act just helped open the Great Plains and the West so more people could settle in those lands.

Those two new territories were still wilderness areas. However, many new people were already moving in to live and start businesses there along the trails—right in the heart of Plains Indian lands.

The Kansas-Nebraska Act did some good things, but it also put more pressure on the Pawnee and the other Plains Indians.

NEBRASKA TERRITORY 1854

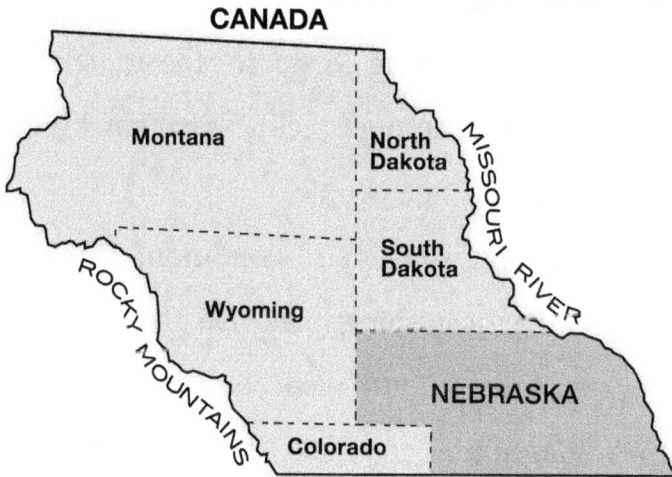

CANADA

Montana

North Dakota

MISSOURI

South Dakota

RIVER

ROCKY

Wyoming

MOUNTAINS

NEBRASKA

Colorado

Map of the whole Nebraska Territory in 1854, as created by the Kansas-Nebraska Act – (This whole area had been the northern part of the Louisiana Purchase in 1803 and the northern part of the renamed Missouri Territory in 1812.) Nebraska Territory, in 1854, contained the current state of Nebraska and parts of the other states listed. Those areas are only marked to show the size and shape of that huge territory and how different it looked from the state of Nebraska today. (Nebraska Territory Map by Ron Lukesh)

Kansas Territory, just south of Nebraska Territory, was also created by the Kansas-Nebraska Act. Kansas Territory then included all of today's Kansas and part of Colorado.

Misunderstandings and Worse

For the most part, the Pawnee who lived along the trails and the newcomers who traveled those trails tried to stay friendly toward each other. But their languages and their cultures were very different. They did not understand each other, and many problems arose.

Without meaning to do so, the travelers also brought several strange sicknesses that killed off many of the Pawnee people.

In their weakened condition, the once-powerful Pawnee sometimes had to beg for food along the trails. They also became easy prey for their longtime enemies in the West—the Cheyenne, the Arapaho, and the Lakota.

Losing Ground

The government tried to keep the peace and tried to limit contact between the different groups of people on the trails. To do that and to protect the travelers, the government added military forts and more soldiers along the trails.

It also held several peace **treaty** signings and bought up most of the Pawnee lands.   Then it moved the Pawnee farther from the trails.

As part of those peace treaties, the American government also agreed to protect the Pawnee from hostile Plains Indians. But that was not easy to do.

For their own safety, the Pawnee had to move closer to their **agency** near the Loup River in Nebraska. That area was where the Skidi or People of the Wolf had often lived.

But even there, because of sickness and continuing raids by their old enemies, the Pawnee tribe grew smaller in number and less powerful. There, the people of the Wolf started to die off.

At the same time, their longtime enemies were gaining more power and new weapons— metal knives, handguns, rifles, and ammunition. They used those weapons against the Pawnee and later against the new people moving west.

By 1857, the Pawnee tribe had only

approximately 3,500 people left. By then, they had sold off all of their land south of the Platte River and even some land along that river.

They were supposed to stay north of the Platte or near their agency on the Loup River. They could still come and go around there, as they pleased. But that would soon change.

The Treaty of Table Creek

In 1857, the Pawnee signed the Treaty of Table Creek. With that signing, they sold off the last of their Nebraska lands except for that small agency area along the Loup River.

That strip of land was approximately 30 miles long and 15 miles wide. (Today that piece of land is known as Nance County, Nebraska.) According to the Treaty of Table Creek, that land would become the new Pawnee Reservation.

The Pawnee were supposed to go live on that land permanently. They would no longer be free to come and go as they pleased. They would have to ask permission to leave there to hunt or to visit relatives who lived elsewhere.

So the Pawnee took their time making that last move.

The Pawnee Agency

The Pawnee Agency was already on the land of that new Reservation. That agency would grow to include an area of government buildings and a town called Genoa. There the Pawnee went to trade and to get blankets, food, health care, protection, and more, from the government.

Other buildings were built there, too, so the Indian agents, missionaries, and other people could provide the Pawnee with schooling, religious training, and job training in such areas as farming, dairying, blacksmithing, flour milling, and other work-related fields.

But the Pawnee were not sure they wanted or needed all of those white men's things.

Pawnee House, a government school at the Pawnee Agency and Reservation at Genoa, Nebraska - Jane North (mother of J.E., Frank, and Luther) and her daughters later worked as teachers or house mothers there. This building once stood near the Genoa Indian School (a training school building) that still stands today as a museum. (Photo Courtesy Nebraska State Historical Society)

Chapter 4

The Norths Move West

In 1855—one year after the Kansas-Nebraska Act opened up that area to settlers and two years before the Treaty of Table Creek—some of the North family came to Nebraska.

At that time, Thomas North and his oldest son James (nicknamed J.E.) left the rest of their family in Ohio. The two of them moved to Iowa, then moved west into Nebraska to find work.

Nebraska Territory was still a wilderness then. There was a lot of work to be done there. There was also a lot of danger.

Thomas and J.E. worked as **surveyors**. They mapped out property lines for towns and homes.

In Nebraska, they signed on to help lay out parts of the new town of Omaha.

Thomas North, father of J.E., Frank, and Luther North
(Photo Courtesy Nebraska State Historical Society)

Thomas also signed a contract to cut down trees and haul the wood away. He was in charge of a 40-man work crew with horses and wagons.

By surveying and clearing that land, he helped make room for the town of Omaha to grow.

The rest of the North family soon followed Thomas and J.E. west to Nebraska.

End of the Road

In 1856, Thomas's wife Jane and the rest of their children came west to Iowa by train. Along the way, their middle son Frank, then about 16, met and made friends with a man named Grenville Dodge.

That meeting would turn out to be very lucky for Frank, because Dodge would soon become an important man with the railroad.

But in 1856, the railroad did not yet extend beyond Iowa City in eastern Iowa. From there, the Norths had to take a stagecoach west and cross the Missouri River into the new territory of Nebraska to reach the new town of Omaha.

A Bitter Winter

In 1856, Thomas and Jane North had three sons: J.E. (age 17), Frank (age 16), and Luther, who went by the nickname of Lute (age 10). They also had two daughters: Sarah Elizabeth, who was called Elizabeth (age 8), and Alphonsene (age 6).

The North family lived in a small two-room cabin in the woods at the west edge of Omaha. Some of the woodcutters who worked for them also lived in the cabin with them.

To make more room in the house, the oldest North brother, J.E., moved to the town of Florence, just north of Omaha. There, he worked at a store where he also sold real estate.

For a time, three families of friendly Pawnees lived in tipis (or tepees) near the North's cabin. Young Lute especially liked those native neighbors. He learned a few words of Pawnee from them in the months they lived there. That would come in handy later on.

Before long, that winter of 1856-1857 turned bitterly cold. Snow piled up six feet deep on the level areas. In some places, it was so deep that wild deer became bogged down in the snowdrifts and could not get free.

The rivers stayed frozen all winter. The family went out every morning to cut firewood and bring in snow or ice to melt on their wood stove. That was the only way they could get water for drinking, cooking, or washing.

So Close to Home

One warm day in March 1857, Thomas North thought the cold weather was finally over. He went out to survey some land along Big Papio or Papillion Creek, a place he knew well.

While he was working, a late-winter blizzard hit the area. Thomas was unable to get home or find shelter in the blowing snow, deep drifts, and bitter cold. He froze to death just a few miles from his home and family.

The middle son Frank then took his father's place at work, clearing trees. Just a teenager, he took charge of the 40 men who worked for his dad and finished the tree-clearing job on time.

Staying Alive

During the next two years, the rest of the North family moved many times between Omaha, Florence, Cleveland, and Columbus, Nebraska. They worked hard just to stay alive.

At one time, the **widow** North even took her three youngest children back East to stay with her family. She did that so her oldest sons did not have to find food for everyone.

The two older boys J.E. and Frank stayed in Nebraska. They lived near Columbus and worked at many different jobs to try to make a living. They cut trees, hauled wood, and delivered supplies to farms, forts, and even to the Pawnee Indian Agency at the town of Genoa.

Frank farmed and broke the tough prairie sod for other people. That was very hard work. One winter, he hunted wolves in western Nebraska for several months. When he returned home, he began a **freighting** business and did some more farming.

J.E. had a farm, too, and he ran a **ferry** boat

across the Loup River. Travelers paid him to take their horses and wagons from one side of the river to the trails on the other side.

Then one day, J.E. and a family friend named Al Arnold heard about a gold rush in Gregory Gulch (now Central City), Colorado. The two of them headed west to look for gold.

Frank followed them there with a freight wagon full of tools, food, and supplies. He sold those items in the gold camps. Then he headed back to Nebraska to work his freighting business.

J.E. and Al thought gold mining sounded like a good way to get rich, but it was a lot of hard dirty work for very little money. The two friends finally gave up and followed Frank home.

Uniting the Families

Late in 1858, Jane North and her younger children returned to Nebraska. They moved to Columbus to be close to her two older boys.

Al Arnold's widowed mother Maria Arnold came west with her. So did Al's brother Ed (also called E.W.), his sister Nellie, and two other sisters. The Arnolds moved into a house close to the Norths. The two families were good friends.

Jane Townley North (mother of J.E., Frank, and Luther North) - She and her friend Maria Rose Arnold (mother of Ed and Al Arnold, and of Nellie Arnold North) were both widows and good friends who came west to Nebraska together. They are buried side by side in the North-Arnold family section of the Columbus Cemetery in Columbus, Nebraska. (Photo Courtesy Nebraska State Historical Society)

In 1859, J.E. North, then 20-years-old, and
Nellie Arnold decided to get married. They dressed
up in their wedding clothes and rode into town on
their horses.

They were married on horseback in the streets
of Columbus. Family and friends stood and
watched from the sidewalks. People talked about
that wedding for a long time.

The town of Columbus was growing, and the
Norths and Arnolds were well liked and respected.
They were honest and hard working and had
earned good reputations.

J.E. North, his mother, and the Arnolds were
community leaders.

So was Frank North, but he was not yet ready
to settle down and get married.

And Luther North was still just a boy.

War was coming to the Plains, and the North
brothers would soon take part in it. So would the
Arnolds and the nearby Pawnee people.

A Pawnee earthlodge village along the Loup River near the old Pawnee Indian Agency and on the Pawnee Reservation. (Photo Courtesy Nebraska State Historical Society)

Chapter 5

The Pawnee War and More

After moving to Columbus in the late 1850s, the North family met many more Pawnee. J.E. and Frank often worked at, or delivered supplies to, the Pawnee Indian Agency at the town of Genoa, about 30 miles west of Columbus.

At the agency, they quickly learned many Pawnee words and customs and made friends with the Pawnee people. Frank was especially good at learning their language and customs.

J.E. and Frank both knew the area well, too. They were good guides and trackers, and they understood how to survive in the wilderness. The Army used them as scouts or as volunteer soldiers when there were problems on the Plains.

Summer of the Pawnee War

The summer of 1859 was a time of Plains Indian troubles. At that time, some settlers said the Pawnee had turned hostile, or unfriendly, toward white people moving in to the area. Newspapers reported stories of raids on settlers and travelers and the theft of horses and cattle.

Reports even said that some white people and Pawnee had killed each other in what came to be called the Pawnee War of 1859. No one knew what to believe, and people were afraid.

It did not help that most settlers in those days could not tell the friendly farming tribes from the more hostile western tribes.

Riding With the 1st Nebraska

After hearing reports of a Pawnee war, one Nebraskan named John Thayer put together a volunteer army. He rode with his 1st Nebraska Army to hunt down the Pawnee and stop them from making war on the settlers.

(A few years later, John Thayer took his army east to fight in the **Civil War**. Later, he would become both a senator and a governor of Nebraska and a governor of Wyoming Territory.)

J.E. North joined up and rode with Thayer's 1st Nebraska Army during that Pawnee War. J.E. understood enough Pawnee words and customs that he could be helpful to both sides.

Man Chief, Head Chief of the Pawnee

During that war, the head chief of all the Pawnee was a man named Petalesharo (Pete uh luh shar o), or Man Chief, of the Grand Pawnee. His good friends respectfully called him Old Pete.

Despite the newspaper reports of a bloody Pawnee war, Petalesharo was a good friend of the settlers. He was a very wise and highly respected leader. He worked hard to keep the peace on both sides.

Back in 1858, Petalesharo had even gone to Washington D.C. as part of a **delegation** to visit the President of the United States at the White

House.   (His father, Petalesharo of the Skidi
Pawnee, had done the same thing in 1821-1822.)

Petalesharo (Man Chief or Chief of Men) of the Grand Pawnee,
head chief of all the Pawnee people during the 1850s-1874,
(photo taken in 1868, six years before his death) - Several
Pawnee leaders had that same name, including his father,
Petalesharo of the Skidi Pawnee, who was very famous during
the 1820s. That common name has led to a great deal of
confusion in Plains Indian studies and Nebraska history over the
years. (Photo Courtesy Nebraska State Historical Society)

In 1858 in Washington D.C., Petalesharo of the Grand Pawnee had his picture taken on the White House steps, along with other Plains Indians. While there, he received an American flag as a gift from the U.S. government.

The Battle at Battle Creek

In 1859, General Thayer did not know if the Pawnee had killed anyone or not. All he knew was that some settlers living in the eight log cabins in the small village of Fremont claimed the Pawnee had done some damage there.

Those settlers said Pawnee horses had destroyed their cornfields. They also said the Pawnee had stolen and killed a cow.

So General Thayer and his Army, including J.E. North, tracked down the Pawnee. They found Petalesharo and his men hunting for deer at a place later called Battle Creek, about 60 miles north of the agency at Genoa.

When the chief looked up from his hunt, he saw Thayer's army riding up, with guns ready. He did not know what was going on, but he feared the worst.

A Quick and Easy Peace

Quickly, the chief dug into his saddle bag and pulled out the American flag he often carried with him. He waved the flag so the soldiers could see it. Instead of shooting at each other, the Pawnee and the white men met and talked about peace.

Petalesharo and the other fifteen Pawnee chiefs were surprised to hear they were "at war" with the white settlers. They told Thayer that a cow had been stolen from some settlers—but not by the Pawnee. They also said they did not know of anyone who had been killed—on either side.

Petalesharo and his Pawnee did not want war. So the chiefs agreed to give up a young warrior who was guilty of killing a settler's pig.

In 1857, those Pawnee chiefs had signed the **Treaty** of Table Creek. At that signing, the Pawnee had agreed to go live on their remaining small strip of land along the Loup River.

That land was to be their reservation. In
return, the government had promised to protect
them from hostile Plains Indians.

In council with Thayer, Petalesharo and his
chiefs agreed to return to their lodges near Fremont
and then to move to the new reservation at Genoa.

Thayer agreed to let them go. The Pawnee
War was over.

A Real War?

J.E. was there with Thayer's Army. He later
told Lute he had seen no fighting between the
Pawnee and the white people. He said that if there
had been fighting, he felt the Pawnee would have
won.

Some historians have said the Pawnee seldom
caused serious problems with settlers or travelers.
When they did, it was usually some of them
begging for food or young warriors trying to prove
their bravery. Other people disagreed with that.

Communications were poor in those pioneer
days. Rumor and gossip were often reported as

truth, and scary headlines made newspapers sell better. So no one knows how much of the Pawnee War was real.

Much of Nebraska and the West was still an unsettled wilderness then. It was a very dangerous place to live—as the North family knew. They would soon be reminded of that.

Chapter 6

Lute Rides the Mail Route

In 1859, the oldest North brother, J.E., had a farm, a new bride, a freight company, other businesses, and a lot of other work to do to make a living. He also had a mail contract.

But J.E. had no time to deliver the mail from one town to another. So he hired his thirteen-year-old brother Luther—or Lute—to carry the mail on the twenty-four mile round trip.

Three times a week, Lute took the westbound mail twelve miles, from Columbus to Leander Gerrard's ranch and post office at the town of Monroe. Then, after a short rest, Lute rode his pony back along those same twelve miles to take the eastbound mail to the post office at Columbus.

Lute would never become a Pony Express rider, as he later wanted to be. But he would ride his pony on his brother's mail route across the Nebraska Plains not far from those Pony Express trails—and a whole year earlier.

Face to Face on a Scary Ride!

Most of Lute's rides were uneventful. But one of those trips in 1859 scared him half to death! He would remember and talk about that ride all his life.

Lute had already ridden a dozen miles that day from Columbus to Monroe. There, he took a short rest stop, as he often did. Soon he was back on his pony and halfway home to Columbus with the eastbound mail.

There was almost nothing along most of that trail—no houses, no farms, no other travelers, just gently rolling hills, prairie grasses, and a lot of sky. Most of the time, Lute was all alone and a little bored, though he really enjoyed riding.

He was half asleep in his saddle on the ride back that day. Then something made his horse stop in its tracks.

The sudden stop almost threw Lute out of his saddle. That woke him up, and he looked around to see what was going on.

There, right in front of him, he saw more than 3,000 Plains Indians, all riding toward him!

Lute did not then know if they were friendly Pawnee or hostile Cheyenne, Arapaho, or Lakota. All those tribes had fought, hunted, raided, and sometimes killed each other in that same area over the years.

Young Lute was alone on the trail— unarmed and afraid—with thousands of Plains Indians riding directly toward him. They had already seen him.

He knew his horse could never outrun them all. And there was no one to help him and no place to run or hide!

Lute took a big chance. He called out a

friendly greeting in Pawnee, saying "How!" or "Nowa!" Then he waited to see what would happen.

Some of the Plains Indians riding toward him laughed. Some of them answered back. Others waved or saluted—then rode past him.

Then Lute began to see dogs and some *travois*, or pony drags, coming toward him. Those ponies had tipi poles strapped to their sides, with the long poles dragging on the ground behind them. Blankets and household goods were draped over the poles, just behind the ponies.

Some women, children, and old people rode on the ponies. Other people rode on the pony drags or walked alongside them.

At that point, Lute knew it was his lucky day! Those Plains Indians were friendly Pawnee— whole families of them—the entire tribe of Pawnee.

They were just moving from their villages near Fremont to their new reservation at Genoa, a few miles from his mail route.

But those Pawnee could just as easily have been hostile Plains Indians from the west looking for trouble. Lute knew he had to be very careful and had to pay attention when riding the Plains.

Winter Fears and Tears

Other dangers also caused problems for Lute on that mail route. Those times, too, made him aware of how dangerous the Plains and nature could be.

Sometime during that winter of 1859-1860, while rounding up cattle, Lute's horse slipped on the ice. It fell on top of the boy, hurting his ankle very badly. But somehow, Lute was able to get back on his horse and get home.

His ankle hurt a lot, and it was more than a month before he could walk on it. Still, he would not quit riding the mail route, even though he could no longer get up on his horse by himself,

For at least a month, J.E. had to lift Lute into the saddle three times a week, so he could make the twelve-mile ride to the Monroe Post Office with the westbound mail.

There, Leander Gerrard had to lift Lute off his horse and carry him inside so he could deliver the mail and warm up. Then, Gerrard had to lift Lute back onto his horse for the return trip with the eastbound mail.

If Lute had ever fallen off or been thrown by his horse, he would not have been able to walk. He could easily have died out there, alone, in the cold and snow—like his father had done—just a few years before.

His mother knew that. Every time Lute rode off with the mail that winter, his mother cried and begged him not to go, but he always went anyway.

Everyone knew that Lute was risking his life carrying the mail. But Lute felt it was his duty to help his family in whatever way he could. He continued to ride the mail route three times a week until his brother's contract ran out in 1860.

Road Ranches on the Trails

During that time, Lute's middle brother Frank drove a freight wagon between Omaha and Cottonwood Springs. Cottonwood Springs was the road ranche near what later became Fort McPherson.

(The term **road ranche** was usually spelled with an e on the end. Road ranches were stores, farms, or small ranches set about eight to twelve miles apart along the overland trails.)

At road ranches, travelers could sometimes trade or buy what they needed on the trail. They could get water for their family or animals. They could sometimes buy food, such as flour, coffee beans, sugar, or bacon. Sometimes they could get medicine.

At some road ranches, they could trade their horses, oxen, or cattle for fresh animals, or get new shoes put on their **livestock**. They might even be able to have their wagons fixed.

Road ranches were like the gas stations and

truck stops along today's highways. They often served many purposes. Many road ranches also became stage stops and Pony Express stops. Later some of them became railroad stations and/or towns.

New Kind of Mail on the Trail

Lute's brother Frank often drove freight wagons along that roadway to the forts and sometimes all the way to Denver.

One day, Lute went with him to Fort Kearny on the Platte River. They also visited the Fort's near-neighbor, the rough village of Dobytown (an **adobe** or sod town first called Kearny City), three miles farther west.

(Dobytown and Fort Kearny were both on the south side of the Platte River across the river from where the newer town of Kearney would be built. The town of Kearney was spelled with an extra e by mistake, by an early postmaster.)

At Dobytown and Fort Kearny, Lute saw his first Pony Express rider and heard about that new mail system. He also saw a poster calling for riders to sign up and ride for the Pony Express. He was very interested in doing that.

Orphans Only!

The Pony Express Company was looking for lightweight boys or young men to ride through dangerous Indian country with the mail. The idea and the adventure appealed to Lute.

While at the fort, Lute tried to hire on as a Pony Express rider. But the station master turned him down, saying he was "too small," "too young," and the job was too dangerous.

Another reason Lute was not hired is that he had a family. The Pony Express Company wanted to hire only young, tough riders who were **orphan**s or who had no close family ties. Life on the trail could be deadly.

A few years later, Lute and Frank came to know at least two Pony Express riders who grew up to be famous frontiersmen—Buffalo Bill Cody and Wild Bill Hickok.

The Pony Express only delivered the mail from 1860 to 1861. After that, regular stagecoach traffic, and then later **telegraph** lines and the railroad, did away with the need for the Pony Express and its riders.

For the most part, the Pony Express was not a major factor in the Plains Indian Wars, but it did add to the traffic on the trails.

Chapter 7

Sparking the Plains Indian Wars

The **nomadic** Plains Indian tribes—the Lakota, the Cheyenne, and the Arapaho—were hunters and gatherers. They did not grow their own food.

Because they lived in large groups, those nomadic tribes needed lots of hunting land. They often had to wander a long way across the Plains to find enough food for their people to survive.

The nomadic tribes did not live in permanent houses. They lived in tipis that could be moved as needed. They often camped and hunted in areas that their people had used for many years.

Sometimes they hunted on lands that other

tribes also used—tribes such as their longtime enemy, the Pawnee people. Often they hunted on lands along the overland trails. All of that led to big problems.

Those three nomadic tribes often got along well together. But they had been at war with the Pawnee and other farming tribes for many years. War was a way of life between them, and they often fought when they met. That was the way they had lived for a very long time.

The nomadic tribes and the Pawnee just could not get along. The same kind of problems would happen between the nomadic tribes and the travelers and settlers moving into Nebraska along the trails from the late 1850s on.

As a result, many battles occurred. Many people died on all sides, and bitter **feuds** developed. Often, one raid or battle led to another, as the people of one group tried to get even for something that had happened before.

Many innocent people were hurt or killed.

That led to even more raids, bad feelings, and problems all across the Plains for many decades.

Sparks of War

Many misunderstandings and problems led to the Plains Indian Wars. But some Plains historians believe one or two major events actually sparked those wars.

The first of those was the Grattan **Massacre** of 1854. That happened at a Lakota camp near Fort Laramie, Wyoming, when that area was still part of Nebraska Territory.

A **Mormon** traveler on one of the trails reported to the Army that his cow had been stolen by the Lakota Sioux.

Lieutenant John Grattan, a young officer, and his **cavalry** from Fort Laramie rode to that Lakota camp. Grattan and his interpreter did not work well together, and the Lakota did not speak English. That added to the problem.

Grattan told the chief to give up the warrior who had stolen the cow. The chief said the cow had not been stolen. He said it had wandered into the Lakota camp by itself. But that message was not understood or accepted.

In anger, a soldier shot and killed the Lakota chief. Other Lakota shot back. Reports say that between 30 and 48 soldiers died that day, including Grattan and his interpreter—and all because of a cow.

The Second Spark

More than a year later, the Army sent an officer named William Harney to Nebraska Territory to take action against the Lakota for the Grattan Massacre.

Harney was a very cruel man. In September 1855, he caught up with a group of Lakota at Bluewater Creek, near Ash Hollow, in Nebraska. There, Harney tried to arrest some of the warriors for the Grattan Massacre. When the Lakota resisted, Harney and his soldiers killed 86 Lakota people—men, women, and children.

Some reports called that the Battle of Ash

Hollow or the Battle at Bluewater Creek. Other people called it a massacre. (Things often look very different through different people's eyes.)

Sparks Continue

Other misunderstandings also led to more problems and more anger and fear, all across the central and northern Plains. Troubles flared up repeatedly along the trails and at western settlements for many years in parts of Nebraska, Kansas, Colorado, the Dakotas, Wyoming, Montana, and other territories.

Very few soldiers were available to patrol that huge area. That left the Plains open to raids and left many people unprotected. Soon major wars broke out along the trails.

There would not be enough soldiers to protect the people on the Plains. And the Plains Indian Wars would not be the only war needing soldiers during that time.

Chapter 8

Wars in the East and West

In the early 1860s, two major wars broke out in the United States and her territories—the Plains Indian Wars and the Civil War.

War in the East

In 1861, the Civil War, or the War Between the States, started back east. That war split the United States in two—the North against the South. (A **civil war** is a war fought by two groups of people living in the same country.)

During that war, people from the **Union** or North states fought to keep the United States one country. They also fought to stop slavery, but they fought about other things too.

At the same time, some of the states in the south fought to break away from the United States. They wanted to form their own country—with their own laws.

The South also fought to keep slaves. Slavery was important for many businesses in the South at that time.

When that Civil War started in 1861, many Army soldiers or "bluecoats" from the western forts were sent east. Most of them fought for the Union, which was also called the United States side, or the North. They often wore the same blue uniforms there, too.

Other soldiers quit the U.S. Army and went to fight for the South or **Confederate States** instead. They often wore gray or sometimes brown uniforms, not blue.

That left fewer and fewer soldiers or bluecoats at the forts along the overland trails. Soon there were not enough soldiers left to protect travelers and settlers along those trails.

There were also not enough soldiers to protect the farming and reservation tribes like the Pawnee.

The Lakota were already making repeated raids on the Pawnee Reservation. They continued to do that for the next several years.

They and other hostile tribes also expanded their raids on the travelers on the trails. As the Civil War raged in the East, the Plains Indian Wars started to rage in the West.

New Laws to Bring People West

During those war years of the 1860s, the government also passed some new bills to bring more people to the Plains.

Some of those were the Pacific Railroad Acts that would lead to the building of train lines west, but those tracks would not actually be built until after the Civil War ended.

Another new law, called the Homestead Act of 1862, was the first of several land ownership laws. That act opened the central and western lands to more white settlement and made farmland cheap to buy, but it still took years of hard work to keep it!

More and more people began moving west to get some of that land. At the same time, there were fewer soldiers on the Plains to protect them. The trails became even more dangerous.

Trouble Along the Trails

Some of the more hostile Plains Indians then saw their chance to reclaim their hunting lands. The hostiles took part in raids on the road ranches, towns, and wagon trains in the Platte Valley and at other places on the Plains. They chased away or sometimes killed settlers and travelers.

In 1862, several small raids occurred along the overland trails and on the Pawnee Reservation. Throughout the 1860s, Lakota, Cheyenne, and Arapaho raids became very common across the Platte and other river valleys.

Fast Ride on a Slow Mule

Luther North experienced some of those raids himself. He had been away at school in Omaha for a while. When he returned home, he went back to work on his brothers' farms and on the Pawnee Reservation.

He also herded cattle for some of the neighbors in the area. On the morning of June 20, 1862, he went out to check cattle and found that all his horses and mules had wandered off during the night.

He found just one mule, so he jumped on its bare back, and rode off to look for the other animals. He thought they would be close. He was not expecting trouble, so he took no guns or weapons with him.

After riding a mile or two around the hills, Lute still had not found the animals. He was about to give up and head back for a gun and a saddle. Then he saw some Lakota warriors ride over the top of a hill and turn toward him.

Lute knew he needed to find safety. So he turned his mule and raced away toward Henry J. Hudson's store a mile to the south. Instantly, the

Lakota started chasing him.

About half a mile into the chase, the warriors saw some Pawnee women working in their cornfields near the reservation. All but one warrior turned and raced toward the women.

The remaining warrior was armed with a long lance and a fast horse. He continued chasing Lute, whose mule was slower. Soon the Lakota rode right up behind Lute and raised his lance to run it through Lute's back.

Just then, the warrior's horse stepped in a prairie dog hole, and the horse threw its rider. Lute kept riding and reached the safety of the trader's store.

The Pawnee women in the fields were not so lucky. All the warriors went after them, even the man who had been thrown while chasing Lute. Nine women died that day in their cornfields, and another one was injured. Lute had been very lucky to get away.

Luther North, about 17-years-old, in the 2nd Nebraska Cavalry
(Photo Courtesy Nebraska State Historical Society)

Lute Joins the 2nd Nebraska Cavalry

In the fall of 1863, the Santee, another branch
of the Sioux, became involved in raids in the
Dakotas and Minnesota. Settlers in those areas put
together their own armies to protect themselves.
Many people were killed there on both sides.

Lute was about 17-years-old when the 2nd Nebraska Cavalry was formed. He joined up and served under Colonel Robert Furnas, who later became governor of Nebraska.

Troops from the 2nd Nebraska went to northeast Nebraska and the Dakotas to protect the settlers. Lute fought in some of the Plains Indian battles there. In December 1863, he returned to Columbus and was **mustered** out of the army.

At that time, older brothers J.E. and Frank had adjoining farms and were doing some freighting. Lute bought Frank's team and wagon and went to work hauling goods and helping with the farms.

Working on the Reservation

Frank then went to work at the Pawnee Reservation store. He quickly became an expert interpreter in the Pawnee language. Before long, he hired on to work for the Indian agent there.

The Pawnee people liked and trusted Frank North greatly. That trust and friendship continued to grow and became very important later.

Around that time, someone discovered gold in what is now Montana and Idaho, another area where many Native Americans lived. Travelers and settlers heard the news. Many of them left the overland trails of Kansas and Nebraska and headed northwest to the goldfields.

More problems arose as those gold-seekers intruded on the lands of the Cheyenne, Arapaho, Lakota, and other Native Americans.

More Sparks

Fearing the worst, the people in the Plains territories enlisted, or signed up, more volunteer soldiers. Many of those men did not understand the Plains Indians or care about their lifestyle, customs, or people.

Few of those soldiers could tell one Plains Indian tribe from another. Even fewer of them could speak any of the Plains Indian languages. That made the problems worse.

That was what happened at the Sand Creek **Massacre** in southeastern Colorado. There, in

November 1863, Colonel John Chivington led an army of 700 men in search of a Cheyenne and Arapaho war party.

The Colonel believed the war party was hiding in a village of friendly Cheyenne and Arapaho people led by chief Black Kettle. The Army attacked the village, killing between 70 and 163 people, mostly women and children. But the war party was not hiding in the village.

Other deadly raids occurred on the northern Plains over the next several years, killing soldiers, settlers and Plains Indians.

Often, it seemed to be more important for people to take revenge against anyone who looked like an "enemy" than to find out who was really guilty and take appropriate actions. There were mistakes and terrible actions done by many people on both sides.

Soon the Great Sioux War was in full force. The Cheyenne and Arapaho often joined with their Lakota friends in raids across Colorado, Nebraska, and Kansas Territories and other areas.

Frank North would be hired to help guide the military men who were sent to that area. Before long, both Frank and Luther North would become important people on the Plains.

Chapter 9

War Stories

In the summer of 1864, Lute crossed trails with a band of Lakota. He was on a freighting trip west to Cottonwood Springs. The Plains Indian Wars were really heating up, but Lute did not know that then.

He was close to Fort McPherson and had not been expecting trouble. But then, a war party of 30 to 40 armed warriors rode into his camp.

Unarmed, and with his wagon horses grazing out of reach, Lute had no way to protect himself or to get away. All he could do was to stay calm and not show fear.

One Lakota warrior rode right up to him. The

man was armed with a bow and arrow. He pushed the arrow point against Lute's chest. Then he drew his bowstring tight to let the arrow fly. There was no way it would have missed going through Lute.

Just then, another warrior rode up and knocked the arrow to the side. As the two men argued about whether to kill him or not, Lute stayed calm and waited.

Finally, the war party rode away, leaving Lute unharmed. He watched the warriors cross the river and move out of sight. Then he quickly hitched up his horses and drove away to safety.

Raid on Plum Creek

A few days later in that summer of 1864, Lute heard that the Sioux or Lakota had declared war on the U.S. government, saying the Indian agents had failed to honor their treaties.

That very same war party that had visited Lute's camp had then joined other Lakota, Cheyenne, and Arapaho warriors. Two days later, they attacked some freight wagons near Plum

Creek.

(Plum Creek Station was a road ranche on the overland trails. It was about 35 miles west of Fort Kearny, and not far from today's Lexington and Holdrege, Nebraska.)

The raiders killed all the freighters in that wagon train near Plum Creek—about a dozen men. The war party also killed or stole all the animals, set fire to the wagons, and took at least two **captives**.

One of those captives was 19-year-old Nancy Morton, the wife of the man who owned the freight wagons. Another captive was a 12-year-old boy named Danny Marble. (They were traded or released the following year.)

That attack at Plum Creek, and other attacks west of there near Julesburg, Colorado, were the opening raids of the Plains Indian Wars of 1864.

During just two days that August, all the road ranches, stage stops, and wagon trains from Julesburg in Colorado to Fort Kearny in Nebraska were attacked. Some raids even extended south down the Republican and Little Blue River Valleys into Kansas.

During that time, an officer at Fort Kearny sent a message east saying, "I find the Indians at war with us...from South Pass to the Blue [River], a distance of 800 miles or more, and [they] have...murdered men, women, and children."

Hearing the news, travelers and settlers all along the trails began to gather what they could carry and hurry back east, back to where they had come from, or back to some kind of safety. Along the way, they heard stories about other raids.

Pinned Together By an Arrow

Some of the travelers hurrying east heard about a raid on the Martin family that same August. That family lived in the Martinsville area, southwest of Grand Island (between today's towns of Doniphan and Juniata) in Nebraska.

At the time of that raid, the men of the Martin family were putting up hay in their fields. Fifteen-year-old Nathaniel and twelve-year-old Robert were helping them.

When the attack started, both brothers were unarmed. To save themselves, they jumped up together onto the bare back of the nearest horse and raced away toward their home.

The Martin boys rode double, as fast as they could, but not fast enough. They could not outrun one of the arrows the war party shot at them.

One single arrow shot into both boys, pinning them together. The arrow knocked them both off the bareback horse, and the fall knocked them out. For some reason, the war party left them for dead right where they fell.

After the war party rode away, the family found the boys lying in the tall grass. The boys were still pinned together by the arrow and could not move by themselves.

They were badly hurt—but alive! They would live to be adults.

Martin Brothers historical marker just off a county road not far from where the two brothers were pinned together by one arrow during a Plains Indian raid on their family's ranch in August 1864. (Photo by Ron Lukesh)

The story of the two Martin boys pinned together by one arrow became a legend in the area. The boys kept the arrow to prove their story and to remind themselves how lucky they had been.

Many other Plains Indian raids happened all across Nebraska, Colorado, Kansas, and other places, as well. Word quickly spread about those attacks and battles. The stories grew, and so did the fears and anger on both sides.

The Great Stampede

Soon the trails became clogged with frightened travelers heading in both directions. A few brave or foolhardy souls still headed west, until the military gave orders to close the trails.

Many more of the frightened people— travelers and even settlers—turned around and headed back east. Some of them even cut their horses loose from their wagons and just rode off— fast—heading back to where they had started from.

Soon, the Platte River trails were backed up with people and wagons all across the central

Plains, from eastern Colorado to Grand Island and sometimes even to Omaha, or into Kansas. But not everyone left.

Forting Up!

Some settlers along the trail chose to stay and defend their homes and families. At Wood River Crossing (near present day Alda, Nebraska), a stage driver named Pap Lamb, his son, and three other men turned their home and station into a small fort. Then they waited, with guns in hand, for the war parties to attack.

About ten miles east of there, at least two groups of German settlers refused to leave their homes at the town of Grand Island.

On the western edge of Grand Island lived William Stolley, one of those German settlers. He and 35 of his friends covered his 20 x 28 foot cabin with dirt and sod to protect it from any fire arrows that might be shot at it.

They brought in food, weapons, and ammunition and turned the cabin into a fort. They put their livestock in the big cellar under the cabin, to keep them safe, while they waited for raids. The settlers called that place Fort Independence and raised an American flag over it.

A few miles east of there, two other German settlers named Henry Koenig and Fred Wiebe turned their O.K. Store into Fort O.K. There 68 men and 100 women and children stood guard or "held down the fort" waiting for hostile attacks.

Other settlers farther east and upriver on the Platte River also decided to stay. They too "forted up" to protect their homes and families. At Columbus, one of those buildings was called Fort Sock-It-To-'Em.

At Elkhorn, they called their building Fort Skedaddle. **Skedaddle** was a word that meant "to run away in a hurry," or "to chase away."

The makeshift forts and voluntary soldiers were ready, but the hostile Plains Indians did not attack.

By then, it was buffalo hunting time. So those

Plains Indians rode off to stock up on meat for the winter instead.

A Call for Action

Later, some people returned to their homes and property along the trails. Others stayed away.

Many settlers, travelers, and newspaper reporters called for the government to do something to end the Plains Indian raids. In response, the Army sent General Samuel Curtis to take action against the hostile Plains Indians.

Curtis was in charge of the Army in Nebraska, Kansas, and Missouri. He and his men headed west toward Fort Kearny on the Platte. Along the trails, they saw many frightened travelers heading east.

They also heard about some brave settlers and their temporary forts. Curtis made stops at those forts in Elkhorn, Columbus, and Grand Island. He later left small cannons at some of those places.

By the time he reached Columbus, General Curtis had an idea. He also had a plan to help guard the area against hostile Plains Indian attacks.

His plan involved Frank North and the Pawnee who had once been the wolves of the Plains.

General Samuel Curtis was in charge of the U.S. Army on the Great Plains during the early part of the Plains Indian Wars in the early 1860s. He is often given credit for enlisting Frank North and the Pawnee Scouts and using them against the hostile nomadic tribes during the Plains Indian Wars. In the mid-1860s, Curtis went to work for the Union Pacific Railroad and was second-in-command to General Grenville Dodge during the building of the Transcontinental Railroad. (Photo Courtesy Library of Congress)

Chapter 10

The Wolves in Blue Experiment

At Columbus, General Curtis went to talk to Frank North and another man named Joseph McFadden who also spoke Pawnee.

Curtis wanted to try an experiment. He knew the Pawnee were always at war with their old enemies—the Lakota, Cheyenne, and Arapaho. He wanted to see if the Pawnee could be used as a U.S. Army weapon against the hostile tribes.

Curtis wanted the interpreters to ask the Pawnee chiefs for a company of men to come work for the Army. He wanted those Pawnee men to serve for one year at a time as volunteer soldiers or scouts with the Army. He wanted them to track any hostiles causing problems on the Plains, and possibly even fight them at times.

Curtis, his men, Frank North, and McFadden rode to Genoa on the Pawnee Reservation. They explained the situation to the chiefs. When they had permission to talk to the Pawnee people, they called for volunteers to join the U.S. Army.

At first, the Pawnee did not understand what the Army wanted from them. When they did, many Pawnee men volunteered to join.

The Pawnee were eager to leave the reservation. They wanted to track their old enemies—and maybe even fight them. They wanted to earn back some respect. They wanted to go back to being warriors, even if that meant they had to follow the Army's orders.

Very few Pawnee spoke English at that time, but Frank North spoke their language very well. The Pawnee trusted and respected him. They also followed his orders much better than they followed McFadden's. So General Curtis made Frank North a temporary lieutenant in the Army.

Frank signed up more than 70 Pawnee men to work as Army scouts that first time. In the next several years, he would sign up many more. Each scout was to be paid regular soldier's wages of about $35 a month, and a little more if the man brought his own horse and/or weapon.

Training at Fort Kearny

Frank North and his Scouts joined General Curtis and his Army. They rode to Fort Kearny for training. (Al Arnold, the Norths' family-friend and in-law was already serving in the cavalry at Fort Kearny at that time.)

The commander and the regular soldiers at the fort were very curious about the Pawnee Scouts. They did not think the Pawnee would make good soldiers—but they did!

That first group of Pawnee Scouts followed Frank North's orders, and they did very well during their training. They rode with the regular Army into western Nebraska and down into

Kansas.   Under Frank North's direction, they proved to be expert trackers and willing soldiers.

Months later, those Pawnee Scouts returned to their reservation to prepare for their winter buffalo hunt and to be mustered out for that year.

General Curtis was pleased with the Pawnee. He gave Frank North permission to **enlist,** or sign up, 100 Pawnee Scouts for the coming year.

Enlisting the Second Pawnee Scouts

Frank rode back to the reservation after the first group of Scouts did.   He signed up 100 Pawnee men at that time.

Chapter 11

Names, Ranks, and Other Differences

Some of the second Pawnee Scouts had been in the first group of Scouts, but it is hard to tell that from the records.

The Trouble With Pawnee Names

The Pawnee had no written language, so in the Army records, the Scouts' names were just written down the way they sounded. But not everybody heard those names the same way.

The Pawnee had at least two slightly different **dialects** or ways of pronouncing the same words. That made it difficult to know how to spell their names.

For example, the word "Bear" (as in the

Pawnee names Traveling Bear and Mad Bear)
might be written and pronounced Ku-ruks or Co-
rux. That would cause problems later on.

Pawnee men could also change their names
once a year, after any special event. So they did
not always use the same name when they re-
enlisted in the Scouts from one year to the next.

Many Pawnee men also used the word Leshar
or chief as part of their names (such as Roam
Chief, Sky Chief, or Knife Chief). They did that
even if they were not really chiefs.

Then, too, some of the Pawnee men who were
chiefs enlisted in the Scouts and served as privates
or corporals under other men who were not chiefs.
That, too, was confusing, but with Frank North's
leadership, it did not seem to cause problems.

Still, all of that made it very difficult to track
the Pawnee men or other Plains Indians through
Army records or treaties or other writings.

Because of all the confusion on names, the
Army sometimes assigned more common names to

some of the Pawnee Scouts to try to make it easier to identify or track them.

White Eagle, seen here as an older man in 1914, was once a Skidi Pawnee chief. He enlisted in the first (1864) Pawnee Scouts using one name and re-enlisted in the 1865 Pawnee Scouts using another name. In between times, he had renamed himself for some special honor or event. He was the first Pawnee Scout corporal. (Photo Courtesy Nebraska State Historical Society)

Some of those scouts kept their new white names or their translated names and passed them on as family names or last names from one generation to another. That made some of the record-keeping a bit easier to track.

Frank North as a young officer in charge of the Pawnee Scouts
(Photo Courtesy Nebraska State Historical Society)

Adding to the Ranks

The Army also made Frank North a captain and told him to choose two other white men to be officers of the next Pawnee Scouts. The rule that created the position of "Indian Scouts" said that all "Indian Scout officers" had to be white men.

Lute wanted to be one of his brother's officers, but Frank wanted his young brother to stay home, do some farming, and protect the rest of the family.

Frank then chose two friends to be his first officers. They were 1st Lieutenant Charles Small and 2nd Lieutenant James Murie. Charles Small had worked with Frank at the Pawnee Agency.

James Murie was a family friend of the Norths. Born in Scotland, he came to America, moved to Nebraska, married a Pawnee woman, and learned the Pawnee language and customs.

(After James Murie and his wife divorced, their son James R, Murie, Junior, went away to boarding school to learn to read and write. When the boy came home, he studied his mother's Pawnee culture and worked with his father's Pawnee Scouts. He wrote important books about the Pawnee history and customs.)

James R. Murie (Junior) with six of his father's former Pawnee Scouts in 1911, many years after the Plains Indian Wars. Back row, left to right: John Buffalo who served with the Pawnee Scouts several times (also called Feather in a Scalp-lock), John Box (also called Fox or Red Fox), High Eagle, and Seeing Eagle (also called They Saw an Eagle) who may have served every time. Front row, left to right: Captain Jim who served several times (Captain Jim was his Pawnee name, not his military rank; he was also called White Hawk), James R. Murie, Junior (son of James Murie, a white officer of the Pawnee Scouts and a Pawnee wife), and Billy Osborne who may have served every time (also called Brave Hawk).

(Photo Courtesy Nebraska State Historical Society)

Frank North also assigned ranks within the Pawnee Scouts as well. A few Pawnee men received the rank of sergeants—below the rank of the white officers. More Pawnee became corporals, but most of the Scouts were privates.

Rattlesnake, a Pawnee Scout – note the corporal stripes
(Photo Courtesy Nebraska State Historical Society)

Off on the Wrong Foot

In early 1865, Captain Frank North brought his two officers and his second group of Pawnee Scouts to Fort Kearny from the reservation.

General Curtis had been very impressed with the Pawnee Scouts as trackers and hunters. But this time, General Curtis was not around. And the officer in command of the fort was not so sure he wanted Native American scouts there.

That commander believed in strict rules. He said that if the Pawnee Scouts were in the U.S. Army, then they needed to look and act like soldiers. He ordered them to learn to march, stand at attention, do guard duty, and keep their uniforms neat and clean—just like regular soldiers.

That did not work very well with the Pawnee Scouts. Native Americans did not stand at attention or march like soldiers. They were not used to being told what to do. They were used to doing things in their own way.

Dressing in Style

Native Americans did not like to dress alike. They liked to dress in their own style. So the Pawnee Scouts made changes to their uniforms.

Driving a Herd, a Pawnee Scout, wearing a plain military coat or bluecoat but with a cloth around his head and a sash around his waist to give it his own style. (Photo Courtesy Nebraska State Historical Society)

Blue Hawk, another Pawnee Scout, who chose to decorate his bluecoat in a fancy style. Note all the metal studs on his shoulders and down his arms and the heavy earrings that were commonly worn by Pawnee and other Plains Indian men at that time. (Photo Courtesy Nebraska State Historical Society)

Some of the Scouts cut ear holes in their Army hats so the hats fit on their ponies' heads. Others decorated their uniforms in other ways.

Sometimes they even rode without any uniforms or with only parts of their uniforms. Most of the time they rode into battle wearing nothing but a **breech cloth** (a cloth worn like underwear).

Brings Herds, a Pawnee Scout – in military uniform
but with his own hat and Plains Indian tomahawk
(Photo Courtesy Nebraska State Historical Society)

None of that made the regular Army men happy, especially when the regular soldiers had to follow very strict military rules.

The Pawnee Scouts did not understand Army orders either. Most of them did not speak English, and they did not see the reason for doing things the Army way. But they would follow Frank North's orders as best they could. They would do what he told them to do and would follow him anywhere.

One of their first orders from the fort's commander was to make a scouting trip on foot in deep snow during a snowstorm. The Pawnee Scouts did that, even though it meant being out in the bitter cold for three days and nights.

When they returned to the fort, there were other orders to follow. One of the next orders had to do with standing guard duty.

"Halt! Who Goes There?"

The Pawnee Scouts on guard duty did just exactly what they were told to do. They stood straight and tall and wide awake for hours at their assigned places, day or night.

When someone made a noise or walked near them, they pointed their rifles and called out in English, "Halt!" But they did not really speak English, so they could not say the rest of, "Who goes there?" Instead, they pointed their guns and would not let anyone move past, until a Pawnee-speaking officer gave the okay.

That worked fine until the commanding officer came out of his office and walked past a Pawnee guard. The guard pointed his rifle and called, "Halt!" The commander told the guard who he was. But the Pawnee understood no English. The Pawnee guard just kept pointing his rifle and repeating the same command, "Halt!"

The commander was afraid he would be shot if he moved, so he just stood as still as a stone— and yelled for Frank North. His yelling scared most of the people in the fort before North could get to him. After that, the Pawnee Scouts were ordered NOT to stand guard duty anymore.

All those things made the commanding officer believe the Pawnee Scouts would not be good soldiers because they did not do things the Army way. He did not see that they would be great soldiers under Frank North's leadership.

Chapter 12

The Powder River War

After their training at Fort Kearny in early 1865, Frank North took his second group of Pawnee Scouts on patrol across the Plains.

Those Scouts expected to patrol the trails in Nebraska, but they and the ones who followed in other years would also range into Kansas, Colorado, Wyoming, and other places as ordered.

Younger brother Lute still wanted to join Frank and the Scouts, but he stayed in the Columbus and Genoa area to protect the family.

A Grand Army

In the summer of 1865, the people of Columbus saw a grand Army of soldiers and their horses come through town. Colonel Nelson Cole's 1,400 cavalry soldiers rode through on their way to the Powder River area of Wyoming Territory. They also brought several **artillery** weapons and a supply train of 140 six-mule wagons loaded with supplies.

Those soldiers were on their way to join up with more than a thousand soldiers from General Connor's cavalry at Fort Laramie. That combined army intended to fight a huge number of hostile Plains Indians causing problems in the Powder River area of Wyoming.

Cole's army seemed to be well equipped, but things did not work out well for him. When he reached the mountains, he and his men could not find the other soldiers they were sent to meet.

Instead, Cole's soldiers became lost. Before long, they were being attacked repeatedly by small bands of hostile warriors.

By September, Cole's army was still lost and had run out of supplies. They had also abandoned their artillery weapons.

Bad weather complicated things, killing 700 of their horses in one night. Lost and starving, the men then had to eat their horses and mules while they waited to be rescued.

Big Magic

During that same time, the military sent Frank North and his Pawnee Scouts north and west. They went to track a war party of Chief Red Cloud's Lakota who had killed fifteen soldiers and stolen their cavalry horses.

The Pawnee Scouts caught up with that war party. During the bloody fight that followed, all the Lakota were killed, but none of the Pawnee Scouts or their officers were hurt.

The Pawnee Scouts then took the stolen horses and joined up with General Connor's cavalry from Fort Laramie. From there, the Scouts led the soldiers to an Arapaho camp of 1,500 people in the Powder River area.

During the battle that followed, Major North

became separated from his Scouts by about a mile. Realizing that the Scout leader was alone, a large party of Arapaho warriors turned and attacked North. He defended himself from behind his wounded horse until his Scouts could get to him. Not long after that, North and the Pawnee Scouts defeated the hostile war party.

In another fight not far away, several Arapaho were killed. Hundreds of horses were captured, and an entire village was destroyed. The rest of the Arapaho surrendered and agreed to go to Fort Laramie to sign a peace treaty.

Amazingly, North was not badly hurt in any of the battles, and neither were any of his Scouts. That made the Pawnee believe Frank North had some kind of magic that would protect him and his men in battle.

New Names

The Pawnee Scouts celebrated their victories over the Lakota and Arapaho by holding name-changing ceremonies. They also decided to rename their leader Captain Frank North. Before then, his Pawnee name had been "Skidi Taka" or White Wolf.

Frank North would not choose a new name for himself, so the Scouts gave him the most honorable and respectful name they could. They called him "**Pani Leshar**" which meant **Pawnee Chief** or Chief of the Pawnee.

Soon after that, the Pawnee Scouts found and rescued Cole's lost soldiers and took them to safety at Fort Reno on the Powder River. Then the Scouts went to Fort Kearny. From there, they returned to the Pawnee Agency at the reservation.

Frank North had his own reasons for going home at that time. On December 24, 1865, he married Miss Mary Smith from back East. They made their home in Columbus, even though Frank was seldom home.

Mary Smith who married Frank North on December 24, 1865
(Photo Courtesy Nebraska State Historical Society)

Chapter 13

Lute Rides with the Scouts

In January of 1866, the government ordered Captain North to enlist fifty Pawnee Scouts for that year. Frank signed up the Scouts and sent them west to Fort Kearny under the command of his friend Captain James Murie.

This time, Lute rode west to Fort Kearny with his friend James Murie and those Pawnee Scouts. Lute was not really one of the Scouts, but he had no trouble fitting in with them.

When he was not with them at the fort, Lute spent much of his time out hunting deer and other game animals by himself. He had a great reputation as a hunter, and the people at the fort appreciated the fresh meat he brought back.

Lute Rides Into Danger

One day when things seemed very peaceful, Jamie Murie gave Lute permission to take ten of the Pawnee Scouts out on patrol himself. During that enlistment, those Scouts carried seven-shot Spencer army rifles.

Lute carried his own single-shot hunting rifle. That weapon was good for hunting but not much good for Indian attacks. It took too much time to reload the weapon between shots. But Lute was not expecting any danger on that ride.

Lute and his patrol rode out looking for signs of hostiles or trouble. They rode for fifteen to twenty miles and found nothing on the trail— nothing but cold and icy weather conditions.

The Scout patrol decided to turn around and head back to the fort while they could. Then in the distance, one of them noticed about 150 hostile Plains Indian warriors riding toward them. The odds were not good—about 15 to 1 against them.

However, the hostiles were a long way off and were mostly armed with bows and arrows.

Outnumbered and Under Attack

The Pawnee Scouts kept a watchful eye on those hostiles as they headed back toward the fort at a steady trot.

Along the way, they rode over some slick and icy ground. There, Lute's horse slipped and fell on a patch of ice. Lute's head hit the ground hard, knocking him out, and suddenly, the battle was on!

When Lute woke up a short time later, he had a terrible headache! He heard gunshots and the screams of injured horses. Looking up, he saw only the cold gray of the sky.

As his eyes adjusted to the light, he began to notice other things. He saw that he was lying on his back on the cold ground, with his head in the lap of one of the Scouts. In one hand, that Pawnee Scout held a rifle. With his other hand, the Scout scooped up snow and carefully washed Lute's face to wake him up fully.

Lute looked around and saw that the rest of the Pawnee Scouts had dismounted from their horses. They had not left him when he fell—and they were not going to leave him. Instead, they had formed a protective circle all around him.

The Pawnee Scouts fired at their enemies. At the same time, the Scouts held the reins of their own terrified and injured horses. Those horses bucked, kicked, and reared up, trying to get away from the gunfire and piercing arrows. Five of the horses had arrows sticking from them.

The Scouts had better weapons than the hostiles, but the Scouts were also greatly outnumbered. Lute knew the Pawnee could have left him to die or to be taken prisoner when his horse fell with him. He would not have blamed them if they had done that.

Instead, the Pawnee Scouts had stayed and risked their own lives to protect him. That was how seriously they took their job. That was how much they loved and respected the North family.

Making a Run For It

Lute knew the Scouts had saved his life. ...But the fight was not over. They were a long way from the fort, and they were not safe yet.

Lute had a terrible headache, but he could not stay there any longer. To stay on the ground meant freezing to death or being surrounded and killed.

As soon as they could, the Scouts helped Lute get back on his horse. Then they quickly got on their own horses.

At a signal, the Scouts turned and faced their attackers and tried to chase them off with more rifle shots. Then they turned and raced off as a group, as fast at they could. Lute rode with them, right in the middle of the pack.

The Scouts rode until they had put some distance between themselves and the hostiles trailing them. But Lute's head was pounding, and he kept slipping in the saddle. The Scouts were afraid he might fall and be killed by his own horse's hooves or by the enemy.

Finally, the Scouts had to stop and let him lie down a while. Again, the Pawnee circled around and stood guard over him.

They fought off another attack, but they knew they could not fight too long. They were getting low on ammunition. Some of their horses were so badly hurt and in such pain that they had to be killed.

The weather was getting worse, and Lute needed rest and a doctor. They had to get to safety. This time when they rode away, they made it back to the main camp.

"Little Chief"

Frank North was very grateful to the Pawnee Scouts for protecting his younger brother. He knew they had risked their lives for Lute.

Frank knew Lute wanted to join the Scouts. He also knew the Scouts respected and cared about both of them. They even called Lute "Little Chief."

Frank knew it would soon be time to let his

little brother become a Pawnee Scout for real.

More Work Ahead

The Central Plains were still not safe from attack. The Pawnee Scouts had many hundreds of miles of trails to patrol and to try to keep safe. They stayed busy patrolling, sometimes with the cavalry and sometimes by themselves.

Very soon, they would also be hired to protect the coming railroad line across the Platte Valley.

Chapter 14

Trails, Rails, and Gandy Dancers

Ten years before—in 1856—the North family had first come west by train to Iowa. At that time, young Frank North happened to meet a railroad man named Grenville Dodge.

Then three years later, in 1859, that same man named Dodge was a railroad surveyor and military man. At that time, Dodge met the future president of the United States—Abraham Lincoln—in Council Bluffs, Iowa. Council Bluffs was then the last train station and the western-most end of the line for the eastern railroads.

A Coast to Coast Railroad

At that meeting, Dodge and Lincoln talked.

They talked about how the United States needed a train line from coast to coast—across the center of the country.

That train line would join the eastern railroad line already at Council Bluffs and would run west. It would go through Nebraska Territory—near the overland Trails—and then on west through the mountains and on to California.

Those two men and others believed that route would be the best one for a Transcontinental Railroad. (The prefix "trans" means "across." So the word **"transcontinental"** means "across the continent.")

Once all the parts were put together, that train line would go all the way across the United States, from the east coast to the west coast. It would go through several states and territories and connect the whole country.

In 1862, President Lincoln signed two railroad acts to start the actual building of that transcontinental railroad. But for the next three years, that train line would not move west of Iowa.

In the meantime, the Civil War was still going on in the East. The fighting there tore up train lines, towns, and countryside—in both the North and the South.

Railroad engineers, construction workers, and soldiers were needed in the East to repair and rebuild those war-torn transportation and communication lines.

General Grenville Dodge was sent to help repair, rebuild, and expand those railroad lines in the East. That would be very important in helping the North win the Civil War and in rebuilding the country after the war.

Near the end of the Civil War, Dodge went to work for the Union Pacific in Iowa. Then he moved across the Missouri River to Omaha, Nebraska. General Samuel Curtis became his assistant with the railroad.

Both Dodge and Curtis had met Frank North years before. They would meet him again soon, and those friendships would grow.

General Grenville Dodge, Civil War general and Union Pacific Railroad man – He met Frank North when North was just a boy, years before North's Pawnee Scouts would protect the railroad. (Photo Courtesy Library of Congress)

Important Link in the Railroad Chain

General Dodge was then in charge of expanding and speeding up the building of the eastern railroad lines to the west. He would be in charge of building that railroad from Omaha, across Nebraska, and toward California.

That train line was very important for several reasons. It could help unite, reunite, and expand the whole country. It would connect all those areas between Iowa and California.

Such a railroad line offered a faster and safer way to travel back and forth across the country than by covered wagon or horseback. Even just one train trip could move more people, more supplies, and more heavy materials faster, farther, and easier than horses and wagons could.

A cross-country railroad would be able to take goods, products, materials, livestock, and even mail from one end of the country to the other in just a matter of days instead of months.

A railroad was also a more comfortable way

to bring families west—especially for women and children—and could better carry the heavy materials needed to build permanent homes, towns, businesses, and schools.

It could also establish stations and links from which to build other train lines to other areas.

In all those ways, the railroad could help tie all parts of the country together.

The Work of Giants

As a soldier and a railroad man during the Civil War, Dodge understood how important railroads were in moving people, livestock, armies, and goods. He also knew how important they could be in the building of the west and the taming of the wilderness.

If the United States were to grow, the country would need railroads to get things moving from one coast to the other. The transcontinental railroad would be the best **technology** of its time.

When another Civil War general, William T. Sherman, heard about the project, he wrote to his brother. In his letter, he said, "If [the transcontinental railroad] is ever built, it will be the work of giants."

The Great Railroad Race

The Union Pacific Railroad started building the transcontinental railroad west, but that was not the only company moving to build such a train line.

The Central Pacific Railroad Company in California had already started building its own railroad east toward the central part of the country.

It would make no sense to have two parallel railroads so close together. So those two railroad companies agreed that they would have to join up somewhere along that route. When they joined, they would form one long railroad line.

In the meantime, those two railroads raced against each other. It was a strange race, because the two companies were not racing beside each other. They were racing toward each other and toward some still-unknown meeting point in the middle.

That race would see which one of those two companies could build the most miles of track the fastest. It became the greatest railroad race in our country!

The Central Pacific in California moved east toward the center of our country. For a while, that company seemed to be winning the race.

The Union Pacific started in Omaha and headed west, but it was slow going for some time. First, the land had to be bought from the government or from some of the early settlers.

The oldest North brother, J.E., worked with the Union Pacific Railroad to locate and buy up land across Nebraska. He looked for land that would make a good trackway for the railroad.

That trackway also had to be surveyed and laid out. The track "bed," or the place where the rails would be put down, had to be leveled. It also had to be made solid enough to hold the weight of heavy moving train cars.

Even on the flatter lands of the Plains or Prairies that took a lot of men doing hard work with picks and shovels and sometimes blasting powder. Dynamite had not yet been invented.

Gandy Dancing

The new Union Pacific's tracks ran parallel to the overland trails. But it would take a lot of long, hard, back-breaking work to build those tracks along those trails. In those days, there were no heavy machines to help, so most of the railroad work was done by hand.

The men had to lift and carry heavy metal rails and wooden railroad ties from big wagons or from train cars at the end of the track. They had to put those rails and ties down in exactly the right kinds of rows and lines to form a track.

Those rows and lines could not be too wide or too narrow or too high or low—or the train cars would not be able to run correctly on them. The rails had to be checked carefully to make sure things lined up.

Then other men brought over huge metal nails called spikes. Some men put spikes in place and held them there. Then other men took turns hammering the spikes in place with heavy sledge hammers. Those spikes kept the tracks from moving or coming apart when the train cars rolled over them.

That work all had to be done carefully and in **sequence** with a certain rhythm, almost like in a dance. **Gandy dancers**—that was what some people called the men who worked to build, connect, and check the railroad tracks.

Many of the gandy dancers came from back east. Some of those men had fought in the Civil War. Others had come from other countries. The Central Pacific in California hired many workers from China to put down their tracks. The Union Pacific hired many men from Ireland to work for them.

The Race Goes On

By mid-July of 1865, the Union Pacific had

built only 40 miles of tracks west of Omaha. Then, for a short time, work progressed fairly quickly, but it soon slowed or stopped when railroad workers reached the central part of Nebraska. There, the railroad had to worry about Plains Indian raids.

That railroad ran parallel to the overland trails and across many Native American hunting grounds. The Plains Indians, especially the more hostile ones, were not happy about so many other people coming across their hunting area and making lines on their land.

Hostiles already caused many problems along those nearby trails. Those Plains Indians were not happy to see the **"iron horse"** of the railroad coming through. As a result, the railroad workers, tracks, and train cars were also in danger during the Plains Indian War years.

A lot of long hard work had to be done to build the tracks across Nebraska and to points west. Those railroad workers could not do the hard heavy work of building the tracks while holding weapons to protect themselves from hostile Plains Indian raids at the same time.

Something had to be done to protect the railroad, its workers, and the travelers and settlers along and near the trails and rails.

Once again, Frank North was called upon to enlist Pawnee Scouts to protect the Central Plains. This time, they would protect the railroad, too.

Chapter 15

Iron Horse and Singing Wires

The Pawnee Scouts stayed busy patrolling and protecting the trails and rails in 1866. They did their job so well, that by late that year, the Union Pacific Railroad was able to put down two or three miles of tracks a day—that was great speed at that time. Soon the railroad from Omaha was a full year ahead of schedule.

The Palace Cars Celebration

In October 1866, the railroad tracks heading west reached a point on the earth or globe called the 100th Meridian. That imaginary or invisible line was near present day Cozad, Nebraska.

The Union Pacific company held a special

celebration to advertise that it had reached that milestone. It sent out two train engines with nine very grand-looking passenger train cars called Palace Cars.

The Palace Cars were not really palaces, but the fancy seats and decorations inside looked very rich and expensive. The Union Pacific invited 200 important people to ride in those train cars.

Those important people were men, women, and children from Omaha and the East. Three of the men came from other countries—one each from Scotland, Spain, and France. Another rider was an American senator, Rutherford B. Hayes. Years later, he became president of the United States.

On the first night of that railroad journey, the train stopped near Columbus. There, more than 100 war-painted Pawnee men held a **mock** war dance as part of the evening's entertainment.

The next morning, the Pawnee held a mock battle, as part of the visitors' breakfast entertainment. There, the Pawnee pretended to do battle with some other Pawnee who were dressed up like Lakota warriors.

After that, all 200 of the important people got back on the train and rode to that 100th Meridian point in those fancy palace cars.

Shooting Photos

The railroad also sent a photographer to take pictures along the way. Photographs were new and very rare in those days.

Cameras were large and very hard to carry around. They were also very **fragile** or easily broken. Such a camera looked like a big black box on tall thin legs. A long black cloth hung down over the back of the box to keep light out.

When that special train stopped at the 100th Meridian, the photographer got off the train. He set up his camera on the ground some distance away.

The man taking the pictures stuck his head under the cloth at the back of the camera. Then he told the people to stand very still for several minutes. The camera took photos very slowly, so the people and animals had to stand very still for a long time. If they moved during that time, their picture would look blurry or very strange.

The camera took pictures on big glass plates. Those heavy plates were hard to carry around. Like the camera, they were also very fragile.

Then the photographer took the glass plates into a dark tent or dark room. There, he spent many hours with chemicals and very little light just to develop the pictures.

That was time-consuming work. Too much or too little of anything—light, time, chemicals, or movement—could ruin a photo.

Finished photos in those days were white and one other color, usually gray or black or a pale brown called **sepia tone**. Sometimes two of the same pictures were shown together in a special holder that created a sort of 3D look to the photo.

"These-Chiefs-Riding"

For the 100th Meridian celebration, that photographer also took pictures of some of the Pawnee warriors. Those pictures honored the Pawnee Scouts for protecting the trains and the railroad workers.

The Pawnee realized that the people in the Palace Cars were important, maybe even chiefs. So the Pawnee called the Palace Cars (and other passenger cars) by a special name. They called them "These-Chiefs-Riding."

The Pawnee called the other train cars **"mules"** because those cars hauled things and were used like work animals, such as mules.

Before long, the Union Pacific would honor the Pawnee Scouts for their service in protecting the railroad and its workers in Nebraska. The company would let the Pawnee ride free of charge in its passenger cars.

The Pawnee could ride from one end of Nebraska to the other (east to west and back again), anytime they wanted, until the mid-1870s. That was when the Pawnee moved away from Nebraska to a new reservation in Oklahoma.

The Singing Wire

As the transcontinental railroad moved west, so, too, did a new form of communication. It was called the telegraph.

Two brothers named John and Edward Creighton from Omaha worked with the railroad and invested money in the company. They also built the telegraph line that ran beside the trails and beside those railroad tracks.

That telegraph line needed many hundreds of miles of telegraph poles and telegraph wire. Those poles and wires looked much like today's telephone poles and telephone lines. But the telegraph worked very differently.

Words did not travel across the telegraph wire. Clicking sounds did. Each series of clicks stood for a letter, and each series of letters spelled out a word or abbreviation in **Morse Code**.

Sometimes, even the telegraph wires made sounds when the wind blew just right. Then the wires seemed to hum or buzz. So the Plains Indians called the telegraph lines "singing wires."

Native Americans knew that white people sent messages along those lines. So to some Plains Indians, the telegraph was an enemy, too.

The Singing Wires sent messages faster than a horse could run, and the Iron Horse or trains brought people to the western lands. So Native Americans wanted to get rid of both of them.

Wherever the railroad went, the telegraph also went. Wherever the trains stopped for water and firewood, railroad stations and small towns grew. Those tracks and trains and telegraphs helped to tie the east and west together.

Things were definitely changing—and changing fast—on the Plains and in the western states.

Chapter 16

A State of Unrest

In March 1867, the people living in eastern Nebraska celebrated something new—statehood. Nebraska was no longer a territory. It was a state, but much of it was still a wilderness, in need of protection.

At that same time, many people in western Nebraska and Kansas, and in eastern Colorado, Wyoming, and Montana Territories, were still worried about more Indian raids.

They had strong reason to worry. More and more people from the east moved onto the old hunting lands of the Cheyenne, Lakota, and Arapaho. More and more white people came. And more and more telegraph poles and railroad tracks lined or cut across that land, angering the western tribes.

Those Plains Indians feared for the survival of their own people and their own way of life. They saw no way to stop that change sweeping across their hunting lands—no way, but to attack the people and things bringing those changes. And so, they made many attacks, and killed many people.

In Good Company

In March 1867, Frank North received orders to enlist 200 Pawnee Scouts to patrol more areas. Those Scouts made up four companies of men, one company for each of the four Pawnee bands.

At the same time, Captain Frank North received a promotion to the rank of major. He also enlisted several more white officers of his choosing—including one captain and one lieutenant for each of the four companies.

He chose men he could trust—outdoorsmen who knew and liked the Pawnee. Most of those

men were friends and family from the Columbus
or Genoa area.

Luther North after he was chosen as an officer of the Pawnee
Scouts in 1867   (Photo Courtesy Nebraska Historical Society)

For one of his four captains, Frank North
finally chose his brother Lute. He also chose their
brother-in-law Charles E. Morse (who was married
to Frank and Luther's sister Alphonsene), another

brother-in-law Ed Arnold (the brother of Al Arnold and of J.E. North's wife Nellie), and, of course, their friend James Murie.

As his lieutenants, Frank chose Isaac Davis, Fred Matthews, Gus Becher, and William Rudy.

Frank North's officers were not always the same from one year to the next, but many of them served with the Scouts off and on throughout the 1860s. Sometimes, Sylvenus "Jim" Cushing (the husband of Frank and Lute's sister Elizabeth) and a friend named William Harvey joined the officer crew as well.

Leading from the Front

The officers of the Pawnee Scouts led from the front. They did not order their Scouts into battle. They rode with them, lived with them, led the way into battle, and fought alongside them.

The officers knew and respected the Pawnee for their courage and skills and for who they were. The officers learned the Pawnee language and customs and would not ask the Scouts to do anything they themselves would not do.

The Scouts, in turn, respected the Norths and their officers. They all worked together as a band of brothers in times of war and enjoyed each other's company in times of peace.

Each time Frank North came to the reservation to enlist men for the Pawnee Scouts, he tried to take the best men for the job. At the same time, he had to turn down many volunteers.

Often some of the Pawnees who were not chosen would follow the Scouts down the trail, hoping to join up or to help in some other way. Some of them did, and worked as horse handlers, wood gatherers, extra guards, or whatever they could—just to be part of the group.

From North Platte to Ogallala End-of-Track

Shortly after enlisting the 200 Pawnee Scouts in early 1867, Major Frank North went east to meet some generals.

His four companies of Scouts headed west to the railroad town of North Platte at that same time.

They were under the command of Captains Luther North, Ed Arnold, Charles Morse, and James Murie.

Spotted Tail and his village of 2,000 Lakota were then camped near North Platte. They had received goods and food from the government. They were not at war at that time.

So the Pawnee Scouts passed them by and kept going west to the end of track near what is now the town of Ogallala. There, the Pawnee Scouts split into two groups.

That year, all four companies of Pawnee Scouts had been issued old muzzle-loading rifles. Two of the Scout companies rode on to Fort Sedgwick near Julesburg. They went there to exchange those rifles for better, newer ones.

The other two companies of Pawnee Scouts stayed at end-of-track to protect the workers and their horses and mules. They needed protection.

A Recycled Arrow

Each day, miles of track were added, and each

day, camps needed to be set up or moved as well. The men could not do such heavy work and protect themselves and their work animals at the same time. More than a few men had died in such raids, and many animals had been lost.

The Scouts stayed busy guarding the many miles of rails and trails, but raids were still common along the line.

Shortly after the two companies of Scouts came to end-of-track, Lakota raiders attacked three miles away and stole 50 or 60 mules. Lute and his brother-in-law Charles Morse took their two companies of Scouts and rode after them.

When the hostiles saw the Scouts chasing them, they ran away, letting the stolen animals go. But one of those raiders was on a slow horse, and he was armed only with a bow and arrows.

Among the Pawnee Scouts at that time was a part-Pawnee, part-Spanish (or perhaps French) Scout and interpreter named Baptiste Bayhylle. He, too, was armed with a bow and arrows.

Bayhylle shot an arrow at the slow-riding raider. The arrow went into the raider's shoulder and poked out of his left side. The wounded warrior grabbed the arrowhead and pulled the whole arrow all the way through his body.

Then he fitted the bloody arrow on to his own bow and shot it back at Bayhylle who was riding toward him. After that effort, the Lakota warrior fell over dead.

Seeing the enemy's bow move, Bayhylle ducked low on his pony's neck. Instantly, the arrow sped through the air, right past where Bayhylle's stomach had been. The arrow just missed him by a few inches.

If Baptiste Bayhylle had not ducked at that moment, he would have been wearing his own arrow through his stomach.

The Scouts returned the stolen mules to the railroad men who held a celebration to honor their return. Fewer raids occurred in the area for a while after that.

Interpreter and Pawnee Scout Baptiste Bayhylle (in back) with four Pawnee Scouts: Man That Left His Enemy in the Water, His Pipe Amongst Others With Great Pride, Curly Chief, and Sky Chief (Photo Courtesy Nebraska State Historical Society)

Exploding Rifles

A few days later, Murie and Arnold's two companies of Pawnee Scouts returned from Fort Sedgwick to end-of-track. Then Lute and Charles

Morse took their companies to Fort Sedgwick to trade in their muzzle-loaders for better rifles.

At the fort, Lute was not happy with the rifles the Scouts were to receive in trade. Those newer rifles were not muzzle-loaders, but they were not new or very good either.

Lute took his time picking out the best of the newer rifles. One by one, he put a bullet into each rifle to see if the bullet would load. In many cases, it would not. Or sometimes the bullet would get stuck inside one of the rifles.

Lute refused to take several of those rifles. That made some of the men at the fort angry. Finally, the general in charge demanded to know why Lute was being so picky.

Lute said that most of the rifles were no good. He gave one to the general so he could see for himself. That rifle had a bullet stuck inside.

The general took the rifle and yanked on it to get the bullet out. The bullet then exploded in the general's face.

Blood streamed down the commander's cheeks, but luckily, his glasses had protected his eyes. Bloody, angry, and embarrassed, the general left the building without saying another word.

After that, no one tried to stop Lute from picking through the rifles and ammunition.

Lute wanted only the best weapons for his men. They were risking their lives to protect the lives of other people.

The general could order new weapons. Lute could not.

The Scouts would need good weapons, as raids continued across the Plains.

Chapter 17

Moving Closer to the Action

One day in 1867, while four companies of Pawnee Scouts were guarding the rails and trails near the end-of-track, a special train came through. On board were Major Frank North, General William T. Sherman (a famous Union general from the Civil War who had become the headman of the U.S. Army), and General Christopher Columbus Augur.

The train also carried several cavalry troops and their horses in railroad boxcars. When the train stopped, the horses were unloaded, and everyone got ready for a long horseback ride.

The soldiers were on their way west to inspect

the new western forts. The Pawnee Scouts joined them and rode along to Fort Morgan in Colorado.

Many of those eastern soldiers had served in the Civil War. They did not want to fight hostile Plains Indians in the West, but they had no choice. They were in the Army, and the Army could send them anywhere.

Guarding the General and His Horses

On the way to Fort Morgan, some of the cavalry men decided to desert or leave without permission. In the Army, that is called **desertion**. It is against the law.

At times, deserters can be punished by being beaten, shot, or put in prison. The punishment is severe, because when soldiers leave without permission, they put other people's lives at serious risk.

One night, the man standing guard over General Sherman's tent deserted—that left the top man of the U.S. Army unprotected in the very homeland of the hostile Plains Indians.

Then too, in the Old West, men needed horses to get around in such a big and wild country. A man on foot was a man in danger, so stealing a horse was a major crime, and hanging was often the punishment for that.

General Sherman had to do something to stop the men from deserting and from stealing the Army's horses. He met with Frank North and ordered the Pawnee Scouts to stand guard over his tent and over the cavalry horse herd.

The General believed he and the horses would be best protected by the Pawnee Scouts. He also sent Pawnee Scouts out to track down the deserters and bring back the stolen horses.

From that time on, while the Pawnee Scouts were with General Sherman in the West, the Scouts stood guard over him and protected his tent and his cavalry horse herd.

For the rest of that trip, few soldiers deserted. Those who did, did not get far.

Moving to Other Quarters

The Pawnee Scouts were first headquartered at Fort Kearny. But as the railroad moved farther west, the Scouts also had to move farther from their homes and families.

After they left General Sherman at Fort Morgan, the Scouts rode north to Fort Laramie and then on to the new town of Cheyenne. By 1867, many of the Scouts were stationed at either the new Sidney **Barracks** (at what became Fort Sidney or Sidney, Nebraska) or at the new Fort D.A. Russell, at Cheyenne.

At that point, the Scouts were responsible for trying to protect hundreds of miles of rails and trails and telegraph lines, and hundreds of people, in parts of three different areas—Nebraska, Colorado, and Wyoming, and sometimes in other areas, as well.

That often kept the Scouts in the saddle for many hours and for days at a time. It also made it difficult to be where they were needed, to stop trouble from happening, but they did their best.

Turkey Leg Tears Up the Tracks

On August 7, 1867, a band of Cheyenne warriors led by Chief Turkey Leg hid out on some islands in the Platte River. They were a few miles west of Plum Creek Railroad Station, not far from today's town of Lexington in Nebraska.

There, the Cheyenne watched some railroad men working on the tracks. When those railroad workers went home for the night, they left their tools at the trackside. A short while later, the warriors used those same tools to tear up the tracks and tear down the new telegraph wire.

Later, when the station man tried to send a telegraph, the message would not go through. Knowing there were trains coming, he then sent out six railroad men on a railroad **handcart** to find out what was wrong.

As the men came near the spot where they had been working, they saw a fire burning in the grass. About that time, their moving handcart hit a break in the rail and jumped the tracks, throwing them off the car.

The Cheyenne then attacked the railroad men, chasing down and killing three of them. The other three workers hid and protected themselves as best they could.

While that was happening, a 25-car freight train ran right into the Cheyenne's trap. The train's wheels hit another break in the track, sending the engine off-center and off the rails. The next five or six cars then crashed into the back of the engine, killing other railroad men.

The surviving railroad workers scattered and tried to protect themselves. One of them walked back up the track and flagged down another oncoming train. That train could not turn around, so it backed up to the last station it had passed.

From there, a message went out over a live telegraph line. It let the Omaha office know about the attack.

The Omaha people then ordered the station

man to get everyone onto the train and to leave the Plum Creek area—fast. They did.

The next day, the railroad company sent men to see how things looked. The train cars had been set on fire and were still smoking. The Cheyenne war party was still there celebrating, but they quickly left when a railroad man shot one of their chiefs.

The railroad workers did what they could for their people who had been hurt or killed in the raid the day before. Then they began to clear and repair the tracks. The railroad would go on.

Turkey Leg Returns

As soon as the Army heard about the Plum Creek Railroad Attack, it sent out a call for Major Frank North and his Pawnee Scouts. At that time, the Scouts were guarding the railroad line 200 miles west of Plum Creek Station.

By then, the Cheyenne chief Turkey Leg and his warriors had already left the scene of the Plum Creek railroad attack. Frank North did not expect the Cheyenne to come back.

Still, North and his Pawnee Scouts put their horses in a railroad boxcar and rode the train back to Plum Creek Station as ordered.

Surprisingly, the Cheyenne war party did return. There they fought a big battle with the Pawnee Scouts. The Scouts killed several Cheyenne warriors and captured some Cheyenne women and children, including Chief Turkey Leg's family, who had been camped nearby.

Later, Major North and Captain Murie held a meeting with Turkey Leg. They traded the captured Cheyenne women and children for white captives and a promise of peace.

Those white captives included the Campbell children, two girls (ages 17 and 19) and their four-year-old twin brothers. Those children had been captured by the Cheyenne at a ranch southwest of Grand Island, Nebraska, a few months before.

The Campbells had lived a few miles east of the two Martin brothers who had been pinned together by one arrow in a raid three years before. In later years, when Lute wrote about this captive exchange, he sometimes confused the Campbell and Martin names.

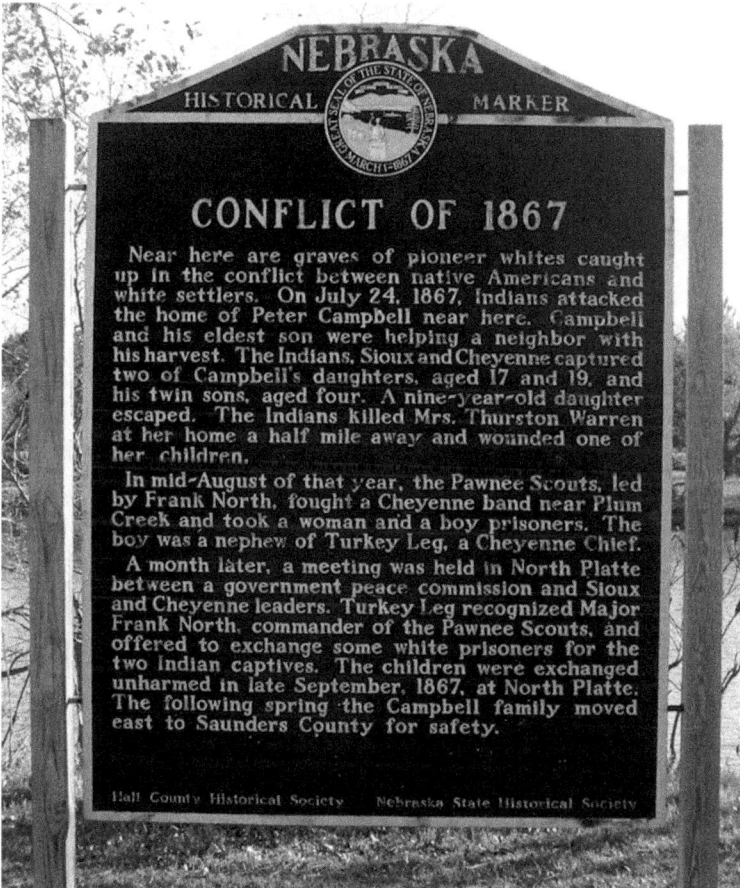

NEBRASKA
HISTORICAL MARKER

CONFLICT OF 1867

Near here are graves of pioneer whites caught up in the conflict between native Americans and white settlers. On July 24, 1867, Indians attacked the home of Peter Campbell near here. Campbell and his eldest son were helping a neighbor with his harvest. The Indians, Sioux and Cheyenne captured two of Campbell's daughters, aged 17 and 19, and his twin sons, aged four. A nine-year-old daughter escaped. The Indians killed Mrs. Thurston Warren at her home a half mile away and wounded one of her children.

In mid-August of that year, the Pawnee Scouts, led by Frank North, fought a Cheyenne band near Plum Creek and took a woman and a boy prisoners. The boy was a nephew of Turkey Leg, a Cheyenne Chief.

A month later, a meeting was held in North Platte between a government peace commission and Sioux and Cheyenne leaders. Turkey Leg recognized Major Frank North, commander of the Pawnee Scouts, and offered to exchange some white prisoners for the two Indian captives. The children were exchanged unharmed in late September, 1867, at North Platte. The following spring the Campbell family moved east to Saunders County for safety.

Hall County Historical Society   Nebraska State Historical Society

Conflict of 1867 Nebraska Historical Marker, located in the Platte River Valley southwest of Grand Island and just west of current Doniphan, Nebraska, not far from the Campbell family graves – This marker tells the story of the 1867 Plains Indian War raid on the settlers nearby as well as the taking of the Campbell girls and boys and their rescue by the North brothers and their Pawnee Scouts. (Photo by Ron Lukesh)

Chapter 18

Close to Home and Down the Tracks

In the spring of 1868, Frank North received orders to enlist another two companies of Pawnee Scouts to protect the rail lines. Frank asked Lute to be one of his captains again.

Lute was eager to accept. He felt it was both an honor and his duty. He admired his brother Frank and loved to work with him.

The life of a Pawnee Scout officer was a perfect lifestyle for Lute. He spoke Pawnee well, respected the Scouts, and enjoyed being with the people. He loved adventure and the frontier way of life and enjoyed being outside. He was also a very good shot and an excellent rider, hunter, tracker, and fighter. He was always ready to go.

However, brother J.E. asked Lute to stay and work for him instead. J.E. was the storekeeper or trader at the Pawnee Reservation then, but he did not speak the Pawnee language as well as Frank and Lute did. J.E. asked for Lute's help, so Lute reluctantly agreed to stay and work for him.

According to a book on Lancaster County history, during that summer of 1868, "all Union Pacific trains starting for the West were guarded by Pawnee Scouts against the Sioux [or Lakota] in Western Nebraska." Frank North and his men would be busy that summer.

Lute would not be with those trains or the Pawnee Scouts, but he would still see plenty of action from home. That summer, Spotted Tail's Lakota also moved east. They began a series of attacks on settlers in the Columbus and Genoa area and on the Pawnee Reservation. Lute and many others from the area stayed busy fighting off hostiles and tracking stolen animals for most of the rest of that year.

Farther to the south, other bands of hostiles from the west made raids across Kansas. They killed or captured settlers and set fires to buildings. Both Frank and Lute North and their Scouts would soon be sent there as well.

Joining the Rails

Meanwhile, in 1868 and into 1869, the Union Pacific railroad moved on west across Wyoming and into Utah. On May 10, 1869, the Union Pacific tracks and the Central Pacific tracks connected at Promontory Point in Utah.

The great railroad race was over. The Union Pacific Railroad had won, and that became the name for that first transcontinental railroad line.

In the years that followed, more and more travelers would choose to travel east and west by train instead of by horse and wagon.

But the Plains Indian Wars were not over. The Army still needed to patrol the Central Plains to try to keep the peace. And the Pawnee Scouts

were still very busy, from Nebraska to Kansas, to
Colorado, to Wyoming, and more.

Map showing the Union Pacific railroad route from its starting
point in Omaha, Nebraska, to Promontory Point, Utah, where it
joined with the Central Pacific Railroad from San Francisco,
California, in May 1869. By then, the Union Pacific Railroad was
already joined with existing railroads from Chicago and other
points in the East, making it the first Transcontinental Railroad in
the United States.   (Map by Ron Lukesh)

Chapter 19

Riding With Buffalo Bill

In early 1869, Frank North was ordered to enlist another company of Pawnee Scouts. Lute joined him and they all rode to North Platte, Nebraska. There they met another Army scout.

That man's name was William Cody, but most people called him Buffalo Bill. He had a great reputation as a pony express rider, a buffalo hunter, and an Army scout. Before long, he would become famous as the hero of **"dime novel"** Old West adventure stories. He would also have his own rodeo and Wild West Show.

At that time, Bill Cody had not yet met the Pawnee Scouts. He did not expect them to be very good at their Army job. But he was quickly impressed by their tracking and fighting abilities when he began to ride and work with them. He would become a lifelong friend and even a ranching partner with the three North brothers.

Buffalo Bill Cody (Photo Courtesy Library of Congress)

Buffalo Bill's sister later wrote a biography about her brother. In her book, she told what Cody thought of the Pawnee Scouts. She said they "were devoted to the white chief, Major North, who spoke Pawnee like a native, and they were very proud of their position in the United States Army. Good soldiers they made, too–hard riders, crack shots, and desperate fighters."

Cody knew that for a fact. He was with them in many battles in 1869 and saw them at work.

Captives from Kansas

The Pawnee Scouts did not just protect the settlers and travelers along the overland trails and the workers who were building the Union Pacific railroad. Part of their job also involved trying to rescue captives taken in Plains Indian war battles.

Most of those captives were white women and children. One of those was Suzannah Alderdice (also called Susanna Allerdice).

Back in mid-1868, the Cheyenne and other western tribes were angry about settlers moving in on their former hunting lands. They were also angry about previous battles with their enemies and about problems with their agents. They went on raids to defend their area, to show their anger, and to prove they were still powerful.

At that time, a Cheyenne war party of perhaps 400 men led by chiefs Roman Nose and Tall Bull made several raids on homesteads in Colorado and Kansas. They burned and destroyed many homes and settlements. They stole horses, killed farm animals, killed many people, and took others captive.

Suzannah Alderdice was in her early twenties then. She lived in north-central Kansas with her second husband and her four young children. (Her first husband had been a soldier and had been killed in battle.)

One day while her new husband was away, the Cheyenne attacked. They raided her farm and killed two of her young sons and later killed her baby daughter. They also wounded her four-year-old son, but he survived.

Suzannah was beaten, tied up, and taken prisoner. She and another neighbor woman were forced to travel with the war party. They were taken to a Cheyenne village in Colorado near a place called Summit Springs. There, those and other captives lived as slaves.

The Battle of Suzannah Springs

Some time later, Frank North received orders to take his Pawnee Scouts and ride to Kansas. Lute rode with him.

From there, they followed the trail of Tall Bull's Cheyenne warriors back to Summit Springs. General Carr and his cavalry rode along, but the North Brothers' fifty Pawnee Scouts would do most of the fighting in the battle that followed.

The Pawnee Scouts would be greatly outnumbered. Still, the Cheyenne warriors would find themselves defeated in a fierce and bloody battle.

But before that happened, and as the Scouts prepared to do battle against the Cheyenne, Frank and Luther noticed someone crawling through tall grass toward them. It was the other captive woman who had been taken prisoner by the Cheyenne in Kansas.

When Tall Bull had heard that the Pawnee Scouts were coming, he had tried to kill her and all his captives so they could not be rescued.

That captive woman was wounded, but she would survive. Suzannah Alderdice would not be so lucky. Luther North later found Suzannah's body, where the chief's family had killed her. Suzannah would be buried at the battlefield. (Lute would accidentally meet and talk to her brother the next year.)

For a short time, that fierce battle was even called the Battle of Suzannah Springs, in honor of the Kansas woman who had been killed there. However, the name would later be changed back to the Battle of Summit Springs, because that was the place-name listed on maps.

Tall Bull would die in that battle, too. According to different reports, he was killed either by Frank North or by Buffalo Bill Cody. Several other Cheyenne died that day as well. The rest surrendered after a big fight and were returned to their reservation.

Pawnee Bravery

During the fighting at the Battle of Summit Springs, one Pawnee Scout was **cited** for special bravery. He killed at least four enemy warriors in hand-to-hand combat in a very short period of time.

That Scout's name was translated as Traveling Bear, but his many friends often called him "Big George." He was a big, powerful warrior, who stood more than six feet tall and weighed more than 200 pounds. He was so strong that he had once shot an arrow all the way through a buffalo. (Unfortunately, no photo has yet been found of that Scout.)

Traveling Bear was a sergeant who often served with the Scouts. He was highly regarded and was a good friend of the North brothers.

During the Battle of Summit Springs, Traveling Bear saw four armed Cheyenne warriors running toward the hills and away from the main fighting.

He jumped off his worn-out horse and took off on foot after them. He ran along behind them and into a valley, with no weapon but his knife. By the time he returned to the other Scouts, he had killed all four of those Cheyenne warriors.

A Mix Up of "Bears"

Frank North and General Augur both recommended Traveling Bear for the Congressional Medal of Honor, for his part in the Battle of Summit Springs. That is the highest award or medal a soldier can receive for bravery.

But Traveling Bear was not the only Pawnee Scout recommended for such a medal in those months. And he was not the only Pawnee Scout with the word "Bear" in his name. That really confused things.

Another Pawnee named Mad Bear or Angry Bear was also a Pawnee Scout with that same cavalry in 1869. Mad Bear had been with another group of Pawnee Scouts working with General Carr's cavalry in Kansas. That was a few weeks before the Battle of Summit Springs.

Near the Republican River, Carr's men had been attacked by hostiles who tried to steal several Army horses and mules. At that time, Mad Bear ran forward and saved the herd, but he was also wounded, possibly by accidental gunfire from the soldiers.

He was not at the Battle of Summit Springs, because he was in the army hospital recovering from the wounds he had received in Kansas.

General Carr had recommended Mad Bear for a Congressional Medal of Honor for his bravery in saving the herd. But the government back East did not understand that two Pawnee Scouts named "Bear" had been serving with the cavalry in Kansas and Colorado in 1869—and both of those Scouts had been recommended for that important medal.

Perhaps thinking that someone had made a mistake, the government sent just one medal—the one for Mad Bear. The army gave that medal to Mad Bear, but Major Frank North was sure it was supposed to go to Traveling Bear.

Some accounts say North took the medal from Mad Bear and gave it to Traveling Bear. Reports do not tell who finally ended up with it—but both men probably deserved the medal and should have had one of their own.

Four Pawnee Scouts from 1869 – Left to Right: Roam Chief, Knife Chief, Charley Brave Chief, and Young Chief (Photo Courtesy Nebraska State Historical Society)

Chapter 20

Peace and War on the Plains

Peace was finally coming to the Central Plains. The last of Nebraska's Pawnee Scouts—or wolves in blue—served in 1870 and were mustered out in 1871. They would be called back into service one more time, but not for a few years and not while they were living in Nebraska.

Guiding the Fossil Hunts

Things were peaceful enough in the summer of 1870 that Frank North also did something a little different. He guided a Yale College professor and his students across the Nebraska sandhills in a successful search for **fossils**. (Three years later, Lute guided the same professor, O.C. Marsh, and his people in another fossil hunt in eastern Colorado.)

1870s Indian Wars Farther Away

By the early 1870s, the Plains Indian Wars were over along most of the rails and overland trails of Nebraska. Still, attacks continued in the northern Plains and from the Dakotas into the Loup Valley.

Frank and Lute worked with the Army and with others in that area to help establish camps and Fort Hartsuff to protect the settlers and the Pawnee in the Loup Valley. (Fort Hartsuff is now a Nebraska state park.)

The Norths also helped start the town of St. Paul and the new Howard County, where Lute homesteaded and held office.

From Heroes to Hard Luck

Despite the new fort, attacks continued on the Pawnee reservation. There, many more Pawnee died of diseases, raids, and other problems.

In the early 1870s, things turned even worse for the Pawnee people. The weather was bad, and crops died of thirst in the fields or were eaten by grasshoppers.

At the same time, new settlers moved into the area, and many of them wanted that reservation land.

Then in 1873, just six years after the Battle of Summit Springs, another Plains Indian battle occurred in Nebraska. And it would have a much different ending.

Many Pawnee would suffer a terrible tragedy, and Traveling Bear, the hero at Summit Springs would lose everything.

Hunting for Luck

By the year, 1873, the Pawnee tribe was in very bad condition. The Pawnee were not allowed to leave the reservation to go on the buffalo hunts that had been part of their religion for centuries. Their spirits were low. So, too, was their population.

Some of the Pawnee people believed they should just move south to Oklahoma. There they could live on a new reservation close to other tribes who were their distant relatives. Those people might be able to help them.

Others of the tribe believed that their luck would change if they could just have a successful buffalo hunt. So they asked repeatedly to be allowed to go buffalo hunting. Finally, the government granted them permission.

That seemed like good news to the Pawnee, but that was probably the worst thing that could happen to them.

A Stroke of Luck

In the summer of 1873, the Pawnee and some young agents headed west on that last buffalo hunt. They traveled the old buffalo trails to southwest Nebraska. There they saw buffalo tracks and knew the herds were close.

They also heard that the Lakota were close, and heard warnings that the Pawnee should turn around and go home instead.

The Pawnee did not want to believe the rumors. They did not want to go home without hunting and without the meat that could feed their people all winter.

They believed that the buffalo hunt would lift their spirits. So they ignored the warnings.

At first, they had a very big and successful hunt. Everyone was in good spirits at that time. There would be meat for the winter. Things looked good. Maybe their luck was changing.

Massacre Canyon

After the buffalo hunt, the Pawnee hunters put away their bows, arrows, lances, and the few rifles they owned. The only weapons most of them had at hand were their hunting knives.

At that time, most of the Pawnee men and women were separated from each other. They were doing different jobs—cutting up the meat, starting cooking fires, working on the hides, drying the meat and preparing it, and more.

While they were doing that, they were attacked by a large war party. Pawnee knives were no match for the weapons of the Lakota.

Many Pawnee died that day at what came to be called Massacre Canyon, near today's town of Trenton, Nebraska. Those who died included chiefs, warriors, Pawnee Scouts, young people and old people—men, women, and children. A few Lakota died as well.

The wife of Traveling Bear and all their children were killed there. He fought bravely and killed some of the attackers, but he was badly wounded.

After the battle, the survivors got away as best they could. Most of their horses had been lost or scattered. So the surviving Pawnee had to walk home. They had to leave everything behind. They even had to leave all the buffalo meat. They would have no winter supply.

Some walked from the Republican River to the Platte River. There a few found safety with people they knew or with strangers.

One wounded Pawnee woman was helped by white settlers at the town of Indianola. She died of her wounds and is buried in the cemetery there.

Along the Platte River, some Pawnee were able to get on the trains they and their people had once protected as Pawnee Scouts—trains that took them closer to their reservation.

Traveling Bear walked home. It took a long time for him to get to the reservation. There, he died of his wounds and a broken heart.

(Today a monument stands at Massacre Canyon, near the town of Trenton, Nebraska. It marks the last major Plains Indian battle between two Native American tribes.)

Chapter 21

Moving South and North

After the Massacre in 1873, the Pawnee people argued a lot more. Some of them wanted to move south to Oklahoma. Others wanted to stay in Nebraska. Finally they all agreed to move.

Between 1874 and 1877, almost all the Pawnee people moved away from their homeland in Nebraska. They moved south to their new reservation at Pawnee, Oklahoma.

Old Pete (Chief Petalesharo or Man Chief) had not wanted to move to Oklahoma. He had tried to convince his people to stay in Nebraska.

During one of those moves to the new reservation in 1874, Petalesharo accidentally shot himself in the leg with his handgun while crossing a river.

A doctor from a nearby town looked at his wound and said it was not serious. Even so, Petalesharo died of infection. Or perhaps, he too, died of a broken heart.

His body was taken back to the reservation. He was buried in the Nebraska land he loved.

The rest of the Pawnee people continued on to their new reservation in Oklahoma, but things would not be much better there for many years.

War on the Northern Plains

While the Pawnee tried to adjust to life on the reservation in Oklahoma, other Plains Indians moved north and tried to survive on the northern Plains. By then, the Black Hills of South Dakota had been given back to the Sioux or Lakota people.

In 1874, General George Armstrong Custer led an expedition of soldiers into the Black Hills. He went to explore the area, but his men also searched for gold and found it on land that belonged to the Lakota. That led to a gold rush there, and to more raids and war.

Lute served as a guide and scout for Custer and his army for a while in the Dakotas, but the two men felt very differently about the Plains Indians. Lute respected them. Custer often said he could beat any and all of them at any time.

Lute did not stay long with Custer. Two years later, in the summer of 1876, Frank and Lute heard that General Custer was dead. He and his men had been killed by a large force of Lakota and other hostile tribes. That happened in Montana at the Little Bighorn River.

To the Plains Indians of the north, Custer's death was a great victory. To the people of the East, it was a massacre. Again, things often look different through the eyes of different people.

News of the Custer Massacre or the Battle of the Little Bighorn reached the East around the 4th of July, 1876. That was America's 100th birthday.

People in the East and on the Plains did not know whether to celebrate the holiday or to fear for the lives of Western settlers.

Scouts Once More

After the Battle at the Little Bighorn, Frank North expected more problems. He asked the government for permission to put together a volunteer Army. He wanted to protect the people of Nebraska. General Carr also asked for the Pawnee Scouts, but the government said no.

Later, when things became desperate in the northern Plains, the Army did order Frank North to go to Pawnee, Oklahoma. There, he enlisted one last group of Pawnee Scouts and their horses.

The Scouts were glad to join. Almost every man of the tribe volunteered, but only 100 could go. And few of them had any horses or weapons. So North received permission to buy horses for them along the way.

In the meantime, the Pawnee Scouts took the train to Nebraska. While riding the rails, they recognized the sites of their old homeland, and they became very excited and happy.

The Scouts got off the train at Sidney Barracks in Nebraska. There they received weapons and uniforms.

From there, they set out for the Red Cloud Agency, north of the Nebraska border but near Fort Robinson.

On the way, Frank North bought horses from some cowboys who were the first to bring herds of longhorn cattle to Nebraska.

Proudly, the Pawnee rode alongside their last three officers—Frank North, Luther North, and the Norths' brother-in-law Jim Cushing. They were the last group of Pawnee Scouts, and once again, they were the Wolves in Blue.

In the Dakotas, the Scouts helped round up Red Cloud's Lakota people and return them to their reservation.

With that completed, the Pawnee Scouts went with General Crook and his men. From 1876 to

1877, they protected the settlers in the northern Plains from hostile raids.

During that military expedition, the armies of General Crook and General Ranald MacKenzie (or McKenzie) consisted of 11 companies of cavalry or horse soldiers and 11 companies of **infantry** or foot soldiers.

That Army also had 400 Native American Scouts, including members of the Pawnee, Shoshone, and Bannock tribes, and even some friendly Arapaho, Lakota, and Cheyenne. Later 200 Crow Scouts joined them as well.

Throughout that winter of 1876-1877, the U.S. Army forces tracked the Cheyenne through the mountains and sometimes fought them there. In November of 1876, the Army defeated the Cheyenne and returned them to their reservation.

In May of 1877, the Army leaders felt they were in control and no longer needed the Scouts. Some fights continued, but the Pawnee Scouts would not be on active duty for those.

Chapter 22

The Last of the Old Scouts

In May 1877, that last company of Pawnee Scouts was mustered out of the service. Frank and Luther North escorted them back to their reservation in Oklahoma.

Those Scouts came back as heroes. They were well dressed and well armed in their own military style. They brought many horses they had bought or won along the way.

A proud but sad group of people they were. Their Scout days were over.

Home on the Range and in the Statehouse

Frank and Luther North returned to Nebraska. There, they and their brother J.E. started a cattle ranch with Buffalo Bill Cody. That ranch was along the Dismal River in the Nebraska Sandhills. Frank ran the place until his **asthma** became too bad, then Lute took it over.

After Cody and the Norths sold their cattle ranch on the Dismal River, Frank North was elected to the Nebraska government from 1883 to 1885.

Frank was in good company. Over the years, his brother J.E. was elected to the Nebraska government twice. Their brother-in-laws Al and Ed Arnold and friends Leander Gerrard and Gus Becher were also elected one to two times each.

Scout's Rest

The Norths' friend Buffalo Bill Cody had another home, in North Platte, too. He called it Scout's Rest Ranch. The Norths, their officers, their Pawnee Scouts, other Plains Indians, other frontiersmen, and important people from all over the world went to Scout's Rest Ranch to visit Cody. His friends were always welcome there.

Buffalo Bill Cody's Scout's Rest Ranch (now a state park) at North Platte, Nebraska – The Norths, their Pawnee Scouts, and others visited Cody here. (Photo by Ron Lukesh, 2011)

Cody's Wild West Show

At North Platte, Cody also started his famous Wild West Show and rodeo. Many well-known frontiersmen worked for him in the show, including Sitting Bull, a famous chief who had been at the Custer Massacre, and other Lakota and Cheyenne chiefs and warriors.

In the Wild West Show, those Plains Indians sometimes pretended to battle with Cody and the cavalry. Other times they pretended to attack a stagecoach driven by Fred Matthews, a former Pawnee Scout officer.

Cody also hired other Pawnee Scouts, and he put Frank North in charge of them. Sometimes North and the Scouts pretended to ride against the hostile tribes.

The Wild West Show traveled by rail to the East coast so people there could see what life in the West had been like. In later years, many of the people and animals in the Wild West Show even journeyed by ship to Europe to perform for the kings and queens there.

The Passing of the Scouts

Frank North rode in the Wild West Show, but his health was starting to fail.

He was always a quiet man. He did not brag or tell people how important he had been in the taming of the West. He gave very few interviews.. Most of the time, he let his actions or his brother Lute speak for him.

Then one day in 1884, a bad accident happened at the Wild West Show while it was on tour back East. In the mess of dust, people, and animals, Frank North's horse threw him. Frank was trampled and seriously hurt.

Although he survived the accident, he did not recover. His injuries, along with asthma and other illnesses, were just too much for him. He returned home to Columbus, Nebraska. There he died on March 14, 1885.

Frank North's home (Columbus, Nebraska) with Stella North Chambers, Stella's daughter Helen Marguerite Chambers, and Stella's husband Edwin Chambers. The house is no longer standing. (Photo Courtesy Nebraska State Historical Society)

Frank North was survived by his wife Mary, his daughter Stella North Chambers and her husband Edwin, and their daughter Helen Marguerite Chambers.

He was also survived by his mother Jane North, two brothers: J. E. (and wife Nellie Arnold North) and Luther, two sisters: Sarah Elizabeth Cushing (and husband "Jim") and Alphonsene Morse (and husband Charles), the Arnolds, other family, even a nephew with the same name of Frank North, and many friends.

Luther North lived much longer than his older brother Frank. Lute continued to live a frontier life and often visited old friends and Plains Indian War battle sites with them. He gave many interviews, and helped write several accounts of his and his brother's adventures.

Lute married late in life, in 1917, to a widow named Elvira Sprague Coolidge. He died on April 18, 1935. He was buried in the Columbus Cemetery, near his brother, in the same area as many North-Arnold family members.

U.S. Indian War Veteran marker – Cemeteries use these and similar markers from other wars to indicate the graves of soldiers and sailors who have fought for our country. It is important to respect these soldiers and sailors (and all graves) and to leave their markers in place and in good condition. (Photo by Ron Lukesh)

In the Columbus Cemetery are the graves of other Pawnee Scout officers as well—the brothers-in-law: Ed Arnold, Jim Cushing, Charles Morse, and friends, like Gus Becher.

In the Soldiers and Sailors Cemetery at Grand Island's Nebraska Veterans Home is the grave of another Pawnee Scout officer. His name was

James Murie, Senior. He was the North brothers' friend from Scotland who married a Pawnee woman.

The graves of other Pawnee Scouts can sometimes be found in cemeteries near the old Pawnee Reservation in Nebraska and at Pawnee, Oklahoma. At least six Pawnee Scouts are buried at the Genoa Cemetery in Nebraska, next to a mass grave of other Pawnee people who were reburied there several years later.

Chapter 23

Pride and Glory

Many people came to the Scouts' funerals. Others honored them through thoughts, prayers, and thanks, for the service the Norths and their Pawnee Scouts gave to the people of Nebraska and the Great Plains—and the lives they saved.

Words of Praise

In 1870, the Nebraska government even gave a special thank you to the Pawnee Scouts "for the heroic manner in which they...assisted in driving hostile Indians from our frontier settlements."

Other people praised the Pawnee Scouts for their part in the Plains Indian Wars, as well.

Donald Danker, a historian who knew the Norths wrote that, "From [the Indian Wars of the 1860s and 1870s] there emerged a striking [group] of fighting men—both individual leaders and troops—around whose names legends have [grown] from their day to our own. Not the least of this legendary company were the North brothers and the Pawnee Scouts."

Army Scout C.S. Mienhall of Callaway, Nebraska, said much the same thing. He had ridden with General Sherman in the Civil War, and with the Norths and the Pawnee Scouts as a cavalry scout protecting the Union Pacific Railroad. He sent a letter to the president of the Nebraska State Historical Society asking the state to put up a monument to the Scouts. (Several other people of that time also suggested a monument to the Norths and the Pawnee Scouts.)

Mienhall said, "We [cavalry scouts] did not see and endure the hardships...that the North Brothers, Major and Lute, did—God bless them and the Pawnees...and [Traveling Bear] the best-ever [tracker]...on the mountain or plain... for their efforts" in making Nebraska "one of the best states in the union to live in."

The President of the Nebraska State Historical Society at that time, Addison E. Sheldon, agreed. He said, "The pioneers of Nebraska owe a great debt of gratitude to the Pawnee scouts and their gallant white leader, Major Frank North. During the Sioux and Cheyenne wars on the Nebraska frontier, from 1864 to 1877, these brave Indians, by their courage and [watchfulness], defended our border, saving the lives of hundreds of settlers. In all the [battles] the Pawnee scouts were at the front. They knew the country through years of buffalo hunting....The story of the Pawnee scouts and their service to the people of Nebraska is one never to be forgotten."

He added, that the eyes of the Pawnee Scouts would always "light up when the name of Major North [was] mentioned, and looking up into the sky they [would] speak with deepest love and admiration his Pawnee name 'Pani-LeShar,'" Pawnee Chief or Chief of the Pawnee.

For the Record

Over time, the deeds of the Pawnee Scouts have been lost in history, but their name and their service to our country should never be forgotten or overlooked.

Hundreds of men served in the Pawnee Scouts during the 1860s and 1870s. There is no way to know how many lives they saved, or how many captives they rescued, or how many miles those Pawnee Scouts rode to do their job.

Because of incomplete records and the nature of the old Pawnee names, there is no way to even know for sure how many of them served or how many times they served.

The Pawnee people may know best about that. They still keep track of who in their family were Scouts. That term Pawnee Scout is still a strong badge of honor among the People of the Wolf.

The flag of the Pawnee Nation or Tribe -- The colors are red, white, and blue, and the small American flag symbolizes patriotism for the United States. The wolf head stands for the Pawnee or the People of the Wolf. The crossed peace pipe and war club stand for both peace and war. The eight arrowheads represent each of the eight wars in which the Pawnee have served as American soldiers, with the first (or far left) arrowhead as the one for the Plains Indian Wars and the Pawnee Scouts. (From a Pawnee flag owned by the author)

The Pawnee Scouts are even represented by the first arrowhead on their Pawnee flag. That arrowhead symbolizes their part in the Plains Indian Wars of the 1860s and 1870s—the first of eight of our country's wars in which the Pawnee fought as members of the U.S. Armed Forces.

The Pawnee Scouts received more than just regular soldiers' wages from their time as Wolves in Blue. They also regained their pride and earned an outstanding reputation. Two of them even earned and shared that first ever Congressional Medal of Honor given to a Native American.

The Scouts returned to their Pawnee people— the People of the Wolf—with stories, memories, some glory, and the knowledge that they had served their people and their country well.

In memory of those glory days of riding with the Norths, many of the Pawnee Scouts—the Wolves in Blue—lovingly kept their bluecoats for the rest of their lives. They wore those uniforms honorably and with great pride.

White Horse (Arusa Taka or Au Sau Taka), a Pawnee Scout, 1870 – One of the most popular Pawnee Scout portraits, this clearly shows a mix of Pawnee and white cultures. In his right hand, he holds a peace pipe/tomahawk—a symbol of both peace and war. In his left hand, he holds a military style revolver. His hairstyle, jewelry, and peace pipe/tomahawk are clearly old style Pawnee, yet the handgun and bluecoat are white culture and military. He is a great example of the Pawnee Scouts or the Wolves in Blue/Bluecoats. (Photo here and front cover, Courtesy Nebraska State Historical Society)

Thinking Questions:
Thinking More About the Norths and the Pawnee Scouts

1. Make a list of some positive character traits that describe any of the North Brothers or their Pawnee Scouts. Choose one trait that you think best describes that person or group and tell why you chose that trait. Compare with someone else's choice.
2. Do research and make a list of some of the often-deadly diseases that came west with the wagon trains. You might also tell some of the symptoms of those diseases.
3. Develop a family/genealogy chart for the North family.
4. Why were road ranches important along the trails and what other things did they sometimes develop into?
5. How did Frank and Luther North and their family develop such a good friendship with the Pawnee?
6. What did the Kansas-Nebraska Act do and how did it affect the Plains Indians of the area?
7. How and why did Nebraska change in size and shape over time?
8. Why did General Curtis think that Pawnee Scouts might work well as trackers and soldiers against hostile tribes?
9. Why do you think Frank North often chose his friends or family to become officers of the Pawnee Scouts?
10. Why do you think it took so long for Frank North to make Luther one of his Pawnee Scout officers?
11. Why do you think the Pawnee renamed Frank North "Pawnee Chief"? Why do you think they renamed Luther "Little Chief"?
12. How did the Civil War in the East affect the people on the Plains?
13. Why did General Dodge and Abraham Lincoln want a transcontinental railroad across America?
14. Why do you think Grenville Dodge and Abraham Lincoln wanted the transcontinental railroad to go through the Platte River Valley instead of some route farther north or south?

15. What do you think General Sherman meant when he wrote that "If [the transcontinental railroad] is ever built, it will be the work of giants"?

16. Choose one of the following things and tell how it changed the West: repeating rifles, covered wagons, road ranches, stagecoaches, the Pony Express, the telegraph, the railroad, the transcontinental railroad, the Kansas-Nebraska Act, the Homestead Act.

17. How did the transcontinental railroad change things for people all across America?

18. Why were there so many Plains Indian problems in the 1860s and 1870s?

19. Why did so many Pawnee want to be Pawnee Scouts?

20. Make a list of some famous people the Norths knew; tell why they were famous.

21. The author repeatedly says that "Different people see things differently." What does that mean?

22. Make a map of the areas where the Norths and their Pawnee Scouts lived, worked, and fought, include such things as territories/states, rivers, towns, forts, reservation, train routes, etc.

23. How did Frank and Lute North help make the Plains a safer place and/or Nebraska "a great state"?

24. How do the Pawnee still celebrate, commemorate, or honor their Pawnee Scout heritage and their part in America's Armed Forces?

25. (Higher Level Question) How did the Kansas-Nebraska Act help lead to the Plains Indian Wars? (Hint: Research the "Kansas-Nebraska Act" and "The Fort Laramie Treaty" with the Arapaho and Cheyenne tribes.)

26. (Higher Level Question) How did the Kansas-Nebraska Act help lead to the Civil War? (Hint: Research the "Kansas-Nebraska Act" and "Bleeding Kansas" or "Bloody Kansas.")

Selected Bibliography

Teaching Resources:
Nebraska Hall of Fame Medal of Honor: Indian Campaigns.
At http://www.nebraskastudies.org/0000/fame2.htm
Nebraska Trailblazers #1 Native Americans, #3 Oregon Trail,
#4 Nebraska's First Farmers, #7 Early Settlers, #17
Notable Nebraskans, and #30 *Kansas-Nebraska Act.*
Nebraska State Historical Society. Available at
www.nebraskahistory.org/
museum/teachers/material/trailist.shtml
NebraskaStudies.org: Nebraska Events and Themes.
http://www.nebraskastudies.org/0500/frameset.html

Nonfiction:
Barnes, Jeff. *Forts of the Northern Plains: Guide to Historic*
Military Posts of the Plains Indian Wars. Mechanicsburg,
PA: Stackpole, 2008.
Broome, Jeff. *Dog Soldier Justice: The Ordeeal of Susanna*
Alderdice in the Kansas Indian War. Lincoln, KS: Lincoln
County [KS] Historical Society, 2003.
Bruce, Robert. *The Fighting Norths and Pawnee Scouts:*
Narratives and Reminiscences of Military Service on the
Old Frontier. Reprint. Nebraska Historical Society, 1932.
Kessinger, 2010.
*Danker, Donald F., ed. *Man of the Plains: Recollections of*
Luther North, 1856-1882. Lincoln, NE: University of
Nebraska Press, 1961.
Field, Ron. *U.S. Army Frontier Scouts 1840-1921.* Elite
series, no. 91. Oxford, England: Osprey Publishing, 2003.
*Grinnell, George Bird. *Two Great Scouts and Their Pawnee*
Battalion: The Experiences of Frank J. North and Luther
H. North, Pioneers in the Great West, 1856-1882, and
Their Defence of the Building of the Union Pacific
Railroad. Lincoln, NE: University of Nebraska Press,
1973.
Manley, Robert N. *Platte Valley Chronicles: Tales from*
Nebraska's Pioneer Trails. Grand Island, NE: Hall County
Historical Society, 2001.
North, Frank. The Journal of an Indian Fighter The 1869
Diary of Frank . North, Leader of the Pawnee Scouts. Ed.

by Donald F. Danker. Reprinted from the *Nebraska State Historical Society Journal*. Literarylicensing.com, N.d.

O'Donnell, Jeff. *Luther North: Frontier Scout. The Fascinating True Story of How the Old West Scouts Made Frontier Railroads and Settlements Possible*. Lincoln, NE: J&L Lee Co., 1995.

Phillips, Thomas D. *Battlefields of Nebraska*. Caldwell, Idaho: Caxton Press, 2009.

*Sheldon, Addison E. "Major Frank North and the Pawnee Scouts." History and Stories of Nebraska. Lincoln, Nebraska: University Publishing Co., 1913. Reprinted Cornell University Library, N.d. Available at http://www.olden-times.com/oldtimenebraska/n-csnyder/nbstory/story30.html

Van de Logt, Mark. *War Party in Blue: Pawnee Scouts in the U. S. Army*. Norman, UT: University of Oklahoma Press, 2010.

Wetmore, Helen Cody. *Last of the Great Scouts: The Life Story of Col. William F. Cody (Buffalo Bill)*. 1899. Reprinted by Digital Scanning, Inc., 2000.

Wilson, Ruby E. *Frank J. North: Pawnee Scout Commander and Pioneer*. Athens, OH: Swallow Press, 1984.

• = Recommended for further reading

Glossary:

100th Meridian: the imaginary line that runs very near Lexington, Nebraska

adobe: mud or clay mixed with grass or straw to make bricks to build a house or other building

agency: the place where Plains Indians went to receive food, protection, and more

artillery: big military guns, like cannons and other weapons

asthma: a breathing disorder

barracks: where soldiers are housed

breech cloth: Plains Indian cloth worn as underwear

captive: prisoner

cavalry: an army that moves on horseback, not on foot (like the infantry)

cited: given credit for something

Civil War: a war between two groups in the same country; the 1860s war between the North and South

Confederate States: the South during the Civil War

delegation: a group representing their own people

desertion: the crime of leaving without permission

dialects: different ways of pronouncing words

"dime novel": an 1800s adventure story that sold for a dime

enlist: sign up

ferry: a boat used to float wagons and travelers across a river at a certain spot

feud: ongoing fight

fossil: the remains of very old plants or animals

fragile: easily broken

freighting: hauling goods as a business

gandy dancer: a man who put down the tracks on the railroad

Genoa (Juh no´ uh): a town now in Nance County, Nebraska; the Pawnee Agency in Nebraska

Grand Pawnee: one of the four bands of the Pawnee

handcart: a cart pulled by hand along the overland trails, often by Mormons, or a small open-air platform that rolls on a railroad track and is moved by two or men pumping a handle

hostile: angry or unfriendly

infantry: foot soldiers

Iron Horse: a term for the railroad

"Little Chief": The Pawnees' name for Luther North

livestock: horses, mules, cattle and other farm animals

Loup River: the river of the Skidi or Wolf Pawnee

massacre: a bloody fight in which many people are killed

meridian: imaginary line on the globe

mock: something that may look true but is just play-acting, such as a mock battle, mock war dance, or mock trial.

Mormon: a person of the Mormon religion

Morse Code: a code made up of short and long clicks (or dots and dashes) that stand for letters or words or abbreviations that are sent over out a telegraph line; named for inventor Samuel Morse.

"mules": Pawnee term for railroad cars used to haul goods or livestock

mustered out: released from the Army

nomadic: moving from one place to another to find food, having no permanent home

orphan: a child who has no living parents

Palace Cars: special, fancy railroad cars used for celebrations and carrying special passengers

"Pani Leshar": Pawnee name for Frank North, means Pawnee Chief or Chief of the Pawnee

Pawnee Chief or Chief of the Pawnee: The Pawnees' name for Frank North

Pitahauerat Pawnee: one of four bands of the Pawnee

Republican Pawnee: one of four bands of the Pawnee

road ranches: rest stops along the overland trails where travelers could sometimes get water, food, mail, or fresh animals, etc.; many of these later became stage stops, railroad stations, or towns

sepia tone: a brownish-color of ink or dye; the color of many early photographs

sequence: in a special order

singing wire: term used by Native Americans to stand for the telegraph lines

skedaddle: leave in a hurry

Skidi Pawnee: Wolf Pawnee, one of the four bands of Pawnee

Southband Pawnees: the Grand, Pitahauerat, and Republican bands of Pawnee

surveyor: someone who maps out the land and helps lay out towns and homesites

technology: scientific advancement

telegraph: an early day form of communication

"These-Chiefs-Riding": Pawnee term for passenger railroad cars

thrive: grow strong, succeed, prosper

transcontinental: across the continent, or from coast to coast

travois: a pony drag; two or more long tipi poles strapped to the sides of a pony and extending backward to drag on the ground. Robes or blankets were laid over the poles behind the pony for easier carrying of household goods or injured people

treaty: a contract of peace

Union: the United States or the North during the Civil War

widow: a woman whose husband has died

Index

About the Author
Dr. Jean A. Lukesh

(M.A.Ed., History; M.A.Ed. English;
Ed.D., Curriculum & Instruction;
Graduate, Denver University Publishing Institute)

Jean Lukesh worked for thirty years as a public school Librarian, Media Specialist, Integration Specialist, Technology Representative, and classroom Teacher. She is probably best known for her popular Reluctant Reader booktalks and American History books. Now retired from everyday teaching, she writes, edits, and publishes books for children and adults, gives history and writing presentations and workshops, and mentors other authors.

Her award-winning *Nebraska Adventure*, a 4th grade Nebraska Studies textbook (©2004, 2005), is very popular with children, teachers, and other adults of all ages. Awards for that book include the 2005 national Texty Award for Excellence in El-Hi Humanities/Social Sciences, the 2006 Nebraska Center for the Book Award, and the 2006 Moonshell Arts and Humanities Council's Children's Nonfiction Award.

Working with fellow Nebraskan Ben Kuroki, Dr. Lukesh then wrote *Lucky Ears: The True Story of Ben Kuroki, World War II Hero* (©2010). That is the first book in her Noteworthy Americans series of Quick Reader biographies for kids 10 to 110. *Lucky Ears* received a 2011 national/international Bronze Medal IPPY Book Award for Multicultural Nonfiction for Children/Teens/ Young Adults and a 2011 national/international Bronze Medal Moonbeam Children's Book Award for Multicultural Nonfiction for Young Adults.

Dr. Lukesh has received many other honors and awards including the Nebraska Library Association's 2010 Mari Sandoz Award.

Wolves in Blue:
Stories of the North Brothers and Their Pawnee Scouts

During the Plains Indian Wars of the 1860s and 1870s, Frank and Luther North and their Pawnee Scouts worked with the U.S. Army to protect travelers, settlers, and transcontinental railroad workers along the overland trails and throughout the Great Plains. Two of those Pawnee Scouts or Wolves in Blue shared the first Congressional Medal of Honor ever presented to a Native American.

Wolves in Blue (©2011) is the second book in the Noteworthy Americans series of Quick Reader biographies. This book is suggested for ages 12 to 112.

****

Sky Rider: The Story of Evelyn Sharp: World War II WASP

In the 1920s a little girl said, "Daddy, someday I want to drive an airplane." She got her wish early in life and grew up to fly almost every kind of World War II plane flown by the Women Airforce Service Pilots. She died young but inspired many pilots for generations to come.

Sky Rider (©2011) is the second book in the Noteworthy Americans series of Quick Reader biographies. Suggested for ages 12 to 112 or young adults.

Lucky Ears: The True Story of Ben Kuroki, World War II Hero

Nebraska-born Japanese American Ben Kuroki was told at an early age that he had lucky ears—and that proved to be true. He fought hard to be able to fight for the U.S. in World War II, and survived an amazing 58 aerial gunner missions against Germany and Japan, then came home to speak for racial tolerance.

Lucky Ears (©2010) was the first book in the Noteworthy Americans series of Quick Reader biographies and won a 2011 national/international Bronze Medal IPPY Book Award for Multicultural Nonfiction for Children/Teens/ Young Adults and a 2011 national/international Bronze Medal IPPY Book Award for Multicultural Nonfiction for Young Adults. For ages 10 to 112.

Go to: **www.fieldmousebooks.com**
to see new books in progress as part of the
NOTEWORTHY AMERICANS
Biography SERIES

Quick Order Information

More Books may be ordered on line at:
amazon.com
barnesandnoble.com

School Orders in Quantity may be made at
fieldmousebooks.com or at
jeanlukesh@aol.com Subject line: **Quantity Books**

For Author Book Talks: e-mail jeanlukesh@aol.com
Subject line: **Book Talks**

"We have **FREE Downloadable Book Covers** and
Award Symbols in Color for Bulletin Board Use."
jeanlukesh@aol.com Subject line: **Covers**

Field Mouse
BOOKS

PO Box 392 - Grand Island NE - 68802-0392

www.ingramcontent.com/pod-product-compliance
Lightning Source LLC
LaVergne TN
LVHW051257080426
835509LV00020B/3028